THE
JESUIT IN INDIA

JESUIT COSTUME, IN SOUTHERN INDIA

THE
JESUIT IN INDIA:

ADDRESSED TO ALL WHO ARE INTERESTED IN THE

FOREIGN MISSIONS

Lives of good men all remind us
We can make our lives subilme,
And, departing, leave behind us
Foot-prints on the sands of time;

Foot-prints that perhaps another,
Sailing o'er life's solemn main,
A forlorn and ship-wrecked brother,
Seeing, shall take heart again.

Let us, then, be up and doing,
With a heart for any fate,
Still achieving, still pursuing,
Learn to labour and to wait.

William Strickland

GYAN

Published by

Gyan Publishing House
5, Ansari Road
Daryaganj, New Delhi-110002
Phone: 011-47034999, 9811692060
E-mail: books@gyanbooks.com

Distribution Network
gyanbooks.com
India, USA, Canada, UK, Australia, France

ISBN : 978-81-212-4531-9 (HB)
First Published, London, 1852

2nd Impression 2020

Printed at: Gyan Press, Delhi.

The Jesuit in India
Author: William Strickland

The Writer has spent four years on the Madura Mission in Southern India, and here describes the past history, the present state, and future prospects of this promising field of Evangelical labour.

By letters received from India since this book was put in the printer's hands, we are informed that two more of our clergymen have fallen victims to climate and privation.

Many valuable lives might be saved by sending the sick fathers to the hills for a change of air—but the poverty of the Mission renders this impossible.

Subscriptions will be thankfully received by Rev. James Brownhill, S.J. 9 Hill-street, Berkeley-square; V. Rev. Dr. Curtis, S.J. St. Fr. Xaviers, Upper Gardiner-street, Dublin; Thomas Barnewall, Esq. Commercial Bank of London, 6 Henrietta-street, Covent-garden; and the Joint Stock Bank, Pall Mall.

W. S.
Missr. Ap. S.J.

CONTENTS.

PREFACE.

THE following little work pretends to no higher character than that of an eye-witness's narrative, and boasts of nothing more valuable than its collection of facts. Whatever reflections the author may have suffered to escape him can be thrown aside by the mind that relishes them not: the history will remain the same.

It is needless to detail to our readers the spirit of a system so well known as that of the Jesuits, or to remind them that, such as it was, its success in bringing Heathen nations at least within the pale of Christianity and of civilization, was equal to what had been effected by any other body. The reductions of Paraguay are well known to all, as one of the most extraordinary successes in the conversion of heathens to christianity ever obtained since the early ages of the Church. The early missions undertaken in the country of which the following pages treat, were likewise considered as a proof of what may be effected by perseverance and self-denial, even against almost insurmountable obstacles. Of late years these missions have been resumed;

with what success may be learned from the following pages.

Our readers will easily here also be able to discern the result of the opposite modes of preaching Christianity pursued at present in India; the one, by everywhere distributing the Holy Bible and sending into the villages Scripture-readers, who can convey its blessed words even to those who know not how to read, and can denounce to them the wickedness in which they have been steeped from the cradle. The other, by the preaching of men, who, with the cross in one hand and the Bible in the other, make Christianity more intelligible than the unexplained Testament itself, and who shew that heathens can be turned more easily from the paths of darkness by tolerating such of their customs as are not absolutely opposed to Christianity, and as far as possible smoothing to them the way by letting them remain Indians, while they cease to be heathens. It is hoped that all who are interested in Foreign missions, all who wish to assist those who are labouring in the vineyard of the Lord, will find here matter for serious reflection, and will ask themselves "am I doing my duty? should all the sacrifice, all the toil be left to others, and shall I not share it with them, at least by contributing my mite to the good work."

THE VICARIATE APOSTOLIC

OF

MADURA.

The Vicariate Apostolic of Madura is situated in the southernmost part of the Peninsula of British India, and contains part of the Southern Carnatic, the provinces of Tanjore, the small, nominally independent, territory of the Tondimau, Marava, Madura, and the country down to Cape Comorin. It is bounded on the north by a branch of the river Cauvery which falls into the sea a little north of Negapatam; on the west by the Coorg chain of hills; on the south and east by the sea. Thus the district extends from about 7·57 to 11·50 north latitude, and in the widest part is nearly three degrees of longitude. The climate is very relaxing, as the heat is almost continual, even in the months equivalent to our winter; but it is usually dry, except in the periodical rainy seasons. The months of March and April, when the sun is going northward, are so intolerably hot that everything that is touched, even indoors, feels hotter than the hand, and exertion of mind or body is most difficult, except very early in the morning or after sunset. The heat often exceeds 100 Fahr. by day indoors, and does not fall above 12 degrees in the night; yet this is the healthiest season of the year. In January and February cholera is very common, arising apparently from the frequent chills, which, though never amounting to cold, are most trying to constitutions enervated by the constant heats. The population may be rated at nearly four millions, partly Hindoos and partly Mussulmen; of the former, about 150,000 are Christians, but the latter uniformly refuse to listen to instruction. The following anecdote will give some idea of their prejudice against Christianity. "A native Christian Priest occasionally visited the College at Negapatam; like our European Missionaries in India, he wore his beard, which his caste among the Hindoos do not, so that at a short distance he looked more like a Mussulman than a Hindoo. One day he came towards the place where a Mahomedan teacher was giving lessons of Telingoo to some pupils of the College; as he came in sight, the teacher eagerly asked who he was? 'One of our Priests,' was the answer. 'But what was he before? was he ever a Mussulman?' asked the *moonshee* with eagerness. 'No, a Hindoo.' 'Oh! well I am glad. If he had ever been a Mussulman I would have stabbed him this instant, though I know I should have been hanged for it.'"

A slight sketch of the creed of the Hindoos, by far the most numerous inhabitants of this large district, may be thought interesting, and indeed will be most appropriate as a preface to our account of the introduction and present state and prospects of Christianity in the Vicariate of Madura.

The more learned and sensible among the Hindoos believe in one only God, called by some Chivem, but more commonly Vishnou. They look on him as almighty, and as the source of all life, as the origin of time, the creator of all, the preserver of all, and at last to be the destroyer of all. They even call him the God of Gods, the only Lord. He is immense, and like the light is present everywhere; he is eternal and born of none, he is all things and will exist in all times, he is infinitely happy, free from grief and care, truth itself; the source of all justice, the ruler and disposer of all, infinitely wise, without form, without figure, without nature or name, or caste or parentage; pure to the exclusion of passion or inclination. He knows himself, and is incomprehensible to all but himself, so that the other Deities, who are but his creatures, do not even comprehend his essence. To him the sun and moon owe their light, and his threefold power of Creator, Preserver and Destroyer are represented in the triple figure called Trimourti. The numberless Gods worshipped by the populace are but imagined for minds too rude and weak to do without material and palpable objects of adoration. All this is distinctly contained in their sacred books, and were it practically held, one could scarcely wish a better foundation for Christianity; but not only are the mass of the people buried in perhaps the grossest idolatry recorded in the annals of the human race, but even the very Brahmins, who profess to believe all they find in these books, draw from them ideas strangely similar to that Pantheism now so rapidly spreading in Germany, and which many look upon as the new form of attack planned by the enemy of man against Christian Europe. "All," say the Brahmins, "is Brahm," (another name of the same Supreme Being described above), "he is the soul of the world, and of each being in particular; this universe is *Brahm*, it springs from him, subsists in him, and will return to him. He is the self-existent Being, the form of endless worlds, which are all one with him, as they exist through his will, which is revealed alike in the creation, in the preservation, and in the destruction, in the movements and in the forms of time and space." It is not difficult to see how inevitably this doctrine must, in uncultivated minds, lead to the grossest idolatry, and such we find to be the fact, for the Hindoos in general have lost all idea of the Unity of God, and have multiplied divinities according to every wild caprice of imagination or passion; some of them being such as decency will not allow the mind to rest on for an instant. Those that can be described may be briefly detailed as follows.

It has been stated that the *Trimouti or triple idol*, is originally but the representation of the threefold action of the one Supreme God, symbolized in the sacred word *Om*, so holy that few will pronounce it, though it is held as the subject of silent meditation; but it usually bears three names: Brahma, the Creator; Vishnou, the Preserver; and Siva or Chivem, the Destroyer; represented as a figure with three heads, and usually three bodies more or less separated. Most Hindoos adore one only of these powers, but some worship the threefold power.

Brahma, the invisible head of the Brahmins, is an emanation of the Supreme self-existent Brahma above described, and the priest and law-giver. He is said to have married Sarassonadi, the goddess of science and of harmony, and is represented with four heads and four arms; in one hand he holds a circle, representing immortality; in another fire, the emblem of strength; with the third he writes in a book which he holds in the fourth, to designate legislative power. Some Hindoos think these represent the four Vedams, or sacred books, which he is said to have written with his own hands on leaves of gold. He has neither temples, nor worship, nor disciples, having by an impudent lie, to be related hereafter, drawn on himself the anger of Siva, who deprived him of the homage of mortals, but his repentance obtained for him the worship of the Brahmins, who pray to him every morning.

Vishnou is more celebrated; he is represented with four arms, riding on the bird Garouda; his wives are Latchimi, the goddess of riches, and Boumidevi, the goddess of earth. The former bore him Monmadi, who is the Cupid of the Greek mythology, and who is armed with a sugar-cane bow, and arrows tipped with flowers, and is mounted on a parrot. He and his wife Radi have no separate temples, but their figures are carved in those of Vishnou.

The sacred books record no less than twenty-one incarnations or *avatars* of Vishnou, but nine of these are especially noted; they are too wild and foolish to be worth narrating at length in this place; in the first he became a fish; in the second a tortoise; in the third a wild boar; in the fourth a monster, half man, half lion; in the fifth a Brahmin dwarf, to humble the pride of the giant Bely; in the sixth a man, to put down the giant Ravanen, King of Ceylon, who made himself be worshipped as a God; in the seventh a man again, to live in solitude and penance, silently destroying the wicked whom he met with; in the eighth once more a man, to teach mortals the practice of virtue and detachment from this world; in the ninth a black shepherd, to exterminate wicked and cruel kings. The tenth avatar is expected impatiently, as the end of the dominion of sin, and the beginning of a new age, in which virtue and happiness will reign alone on earth. Ridiculous as are these transformations, their details would be far more so, yet one finds in them many points of resemblance with the history of our Lord and Saviour, so striking as to leave no doubt of their being borrowed from Christianity.

Vishnou is the second person of their Trinity, taking flesh to free the world from evil, which had spread so widely as to touch him with pity. He says in one place, "Though by nature not subject to be born or to die, though I rule all creation, I yet command my own nature, and make myself visible by my own power, and as often as virtue becomes weak in the world, and vice and injustice rise up, so often I am seen. Thus I appear from age to age to save the just, destroy the wicked and re-establish tottering virtue." He came on earth by a sacrifice of which he alone was capable, to save it from certain destruction; he subjected himself to all the weaknesses and miseries of humanity, and to a cruel death to destroy evil, and to make virtue reign; he became a shepherd, a warrior, and a prophet, to leave a pattern to mankind, yet he is all the time the God of all, the representative of the invisible Being by whom he was sent, and powerful, just, good and merciful like him; compassionate even to his enemies, and requiring from his followers faith and love, and a true and spiritual worship, a desire of being united to him, self-denial and a contempt of the world; he alone can make people holy, and give eternal happiness. Here again we have ideas which would make the introduction of Christianity easy were they really current among the people, but unfortunately they are known only to the more learned among them, and even with them have little influence on their practice, they are therefore no check to the grossest idolatry and all its consequences of systematized sensuality. To continue our sketch of their better known fables —Brahma and Vishnou were struggling for preeminence, and the universe shook with the combat, when the Supreme God appeared in the form of an endless column of fire, and terrified, they paused. He promised superiority to whichever should first find the extremity of this column, and Vishnou, in the form of a wild boar, spent a thousand years in digging, but in vain. Brahma meanwhile, in the form of a swan, soared upwards for 100,000 years, but without success; tired he went to Vishnou, and told him he had reached the summit of the column, showing as proof, a flower, which spoke and confirmed his falsehood; but the column opened, the eight elephants who support the earth spouted blood, the clouds were burned, and the Supreme God appeared, laughing derisively, and cursing Brahma, who cast himself at Siva's feet, and received pardon so far as to be worshipped by the Brahmins. Had we space we might multiply such tales almost infinitely, but we have said enough to excite the gratitude of those to whom truth has been revealed, and to make them pity the millions who are buried in such gross darkness. A petrified shell, called Salagranan, is often worshipped as an idol of Vishnou, because it sometimes has nine different shades of colour, which are considered emblems of these nine avatars. It is carried in a white linen cloth, with the greatest respect, bathed with many ceremonies, and the water is drunk as a means of purification.

Siva, the third God of the Trimourti, has two opposite aspects: under the names of Bhava, Baghis, Bhogovan, &c., he is the father and benefactor of all, his forehead is adorned with a crescent, he rides on the bull Nandi, and holds in his hands the lotus and the good serpent; but under the names of Cala, Hara, Ougra, &c., he seems to change his nature: he is the god of destruction, the conqueror of death and of demons, fearful of aspect, with long sharp teeth, flames for hair, and human skulls for a necklace, while his girdle, and the bracelets of his many arms, are fierce serpents. He delights in blood and tears and in the most cruel vengeance, and he rides a tiger. The Hindoos of his sect look on him as the only God, and give him a wife named Parvati, who resembles the Phrygian Cybele: she is often worshipped together with him, but sometimes has separate temples.

Their son Pollear presides over marriages; he is represented under the most monstrous forms, and is so venerated that his image appears in every temple, under trees, by the road sides, and our missionaries have sometimes difficulty in dissuading Christian women from wearing it among their ornaments. But we cannot pursue to their full extent the degrading idolatries of these poor people; their divinities have been said to amount to 33,000, and many animals are among the number; especially the monkey, for whom the worshippers of Vishnou have a peculiar regard, so much so that they consider it a most meritorious act to give him food, and they salam * to him every morning when they first meet him. The Garouda, or Malabar eagle, is also adored by Vishnou's followers, and on the holy day that we Christians give to the divine worship, they often meet to adore the Garoudas, and feed them with meat. To kill one of them would be considered a crime equal to manslaughter. Siva's followers venerate the bull, which is sacred all over India. The serpent too, espe-

* Salam is originally a Turkish word, and is a general word of salutation of the Mussulman population in India. The term is in some measure adopted by the Hindoos, and the way of offering it is different according to the caste of the person performing it and the rank of the person receiving it.

cially the cobra capella, is held in great respect; temples are erected to these reptiles, and those which find their way into houses often receive sacrifices, and what they prefer, food. But not content with adoring brute creatures, they make gods of rough stones. Frequently, in travelling through the country, one may perceive a number of rough stones arranged in a straight line or a circle by some devotee, who has rubbed them over with saffron; another takes it into his head to offer up a sacrifice of a cock or a lamb to these stones, and smears them over with the blood; this is sufficient to render these stones holy in the eyes of the neighbouring people, who immediately begin to worship them, and perhaps before long some rich native builds a temple on the spot. Such has been the origin of many of the most famous temples in India. Others have arisen from a suniassi, or penitent, affixing a rag of his clothes to a bush, in token of the holy emotion he felt accidentally in the spot; seeing this, others imitate his example, and soon the bush is counted sacred, and all hung with rags; a stone is placed before it, reddened with the juice of the betel nut; perhaps a wall is built around, and if a rich man take a fancy to build a temple there, idle Brahmins will crowd to it, festivals will be held, and it becomes a celebrated place.

Many Europeans would willingly persuade themselves that all this is but symbolical, and that God is thus honoured in His works; the testimony of the learned Brahmin Ramohim Roy should be conclusive to the contrary. He devoted much time to the study of Hindooism, in order to assist in the propagation of that Christianity which he cannot be said to have himself learned, since he died a Unitarian, but in his endeavours to convince his countrymen of the folly of idolatry, he showed the additions continually made by the Brahmins to their sacred books, and he testifies to the complete forgetfulness of all idea of one Supreme Being. He says they do not look on their idols as emblems of Him or His power, but firmly believe in the reality of their numberless gods and goddesses, all possessing complete and independent power; to make them propitious, the temples are erected, and the ceremonies performed, and it would be considered a heresy to think otherwise.

The morality of their sacred books is higher

than would be supposed from the preceding sketch, and in several respects approaches to the Christian law. They require prayer, fasting, works of benevolence, patience in suffering. Frequent bathing, which in such a climate is necessary for health, is also enjoined. In the details regarding the obligations of each caste, are some wise regulations, mingled with much foolish superstition. Those who execute works useful to the public, such as tanks, temples, places of shelter for travellers, will be reckoned among the good and rewarded; those who burn with love and wisdom will go to the heaven of Brahma himself, and will share the delights of the gods. The wicked will endure indescribable torments: those who are disrespectful to their parents, or to the Brahmins, will burn in fire; calumniators and slanderers will be stretched on beds of red hot iron, and forced to feed on ordure; the voluptuous, the indolent, and the hard-hearted will be cast into burning caverns, and trampled by elephants, who will feed on their flesh. But these torments, though of immense duration, will not be eternal; at length their bodies will be resuscitated, and they will live again, unless they have drunk of the water of the Ganges, which exempts from a fresh trial of this painful life. The reward of the good will never end.

They believe in the doctrine of metempsychosis, that is, the transmigration of souls; they think that, after more or less punishment, a soul will live again in a form suited to its deserts, rich or poor, of high or low caste, often even that of a beast, and therefore many of the natives will not destroy life in any shape. Before the introduction of this doctrine, there is no doubt that human sacrifices had been offered in all parts of India; now they shew their devotion to their gods and goddesses by offerings of fruits and flowers, works of penance, or of usefulness to their fellow creatures, and splendid festivals in honour of their divinities. The magnificence of their temples, and the riches amassed in them, are perfectly astonishing. Among other ceremonies of their festivals, the idol is sometimes placed on an enormous car, and dragged in procession through the streets, and fanatics have frequently been known to throw themselves before this chariot, that they might be crushed under its wheels. This has however become rare of late years, in consequence of the active interference of the British government, and the number of pilgrims has consequently very much diminished.

Europeans who think so much of the light and easy practices required or recommended by Catholicity to remind us of the sufferings of Christ, would hardly believe what the Hindoos endure in honour of their false gods. Some will, at certain festivals, allow themselves to be suspended from a height by iron hooks passed through the muscles of the back; others will walk on burning embers barefoot; some go almost or quite naked, wandering about, eating only enough to preserve life, and subsisting on alms; others have made a vow of silence; some travel about bearing Ganges water, others dancing and singing the praises of Vishnou; some penitents tear themselves with whips, or have themselves chained for life to the foot of a tree, or preserve for years some painful attitude, such as holding their arms raised above their heads so that they cannot feed themselves, or keeping the hands clenched till the nails have been known to grow out through the palm to the back. But it would be endless to relate the ingenious tortures which are practised by these unhappy creatures, and in which they glory, considering themselves happy beyond all others, and exalted by their performance. The custom of Suttee, or the burning of widows on the funeral pile of their deceased husbands, need not here be alluded to, as the English government make every effort to check it, and for many years it has ceased in the South of India, with which our Mission is principally interested. Of the frightful licentiousness authorized and encouraged under the name of religion we will not speak—but nothing in the annals of heathen Greece or Rome, nothing among the practices of the early heretics exceeded it.

A brief mention of the castes into which the Hindoos are well known to be divided may be interesting. The chief of these are the Brahmins, said to have sprung from the head of Brahma, and therefore superior to all others, and enjoying many privileges. They are considered the interpreters of the gods, and are the depositaries of all knowledge, but they usually lead a very idle and evil life. Many of them hold small civil appointments under the English Government, and they are certainly the cleverest and most intriguing race in India, but comparatively few of them have become Christians. The next caste is that of the Chatrias, or warriors, who are said to have sprung from the arms of Brahma; then the Vissias, labourers and merchants, who came from his body; and the Soudas, or artisans, from his feet. The names of the castes vary somewhat in different parts of the country: in Madura, the next to the Brahmins are the Moodeliars and Vellalers, and some of both castes have become Christians,—some of them even are among the most fervent. Their rank makes them very useful as an encouragement to others. After them come the Maravers, who are considered noble, and among whom many were converted by the early Missionaries; but latterly the entire privation of spiritual instruction and aid, and the violence of evil passions, have made most of them relapse into idolatry. They are the robber caste—fierce and harsh. Their numbers have rapidly diminished, and they are not now a large caste, or by any means rich. The Odiages, or labourers, rank next, and are both numerous and wealthy. And there are several lesser divisions before we reach the lowest class of all—the wretched, despised Paria. All these castes are subdivided, as the different names which one caste frequently bears will sufficiently indicate. The Soudras are the most numerous, and the subdivisions of this caste are endless. Every one is obliged to follow the calling of his father. Military service, commerce, agriculture, and weaving, are honoured in all castes; and the three first may be followed even by Brahmins, while the Paria is not forbidden to weave. There are priests in every caste as well as among the Brahmins. There are many tribes not counted as castes at all; the chief of which is the *outcast* tribe—called Paria: they form one-fourth of the whole population, and are almost universally looked down upon and shunned. Some think them the remains of a conquered nation, the original inhabitants of the country; but it is much more probable that they consist of persons whose ancestors were banished for crimes from the other castes. Some of them are intelligent, and contrive to amass considerable wealth: from amongst them Europeans take the greater number of their servants; which fact alone has immensely contributed to the prejudices of the higher castes against Europeans and their creed. The excessive humiliation to which they used to be subjected by the superior castes is wearing away rapidly. It would be impossible here to enter into the many minor details of these great divisions.

There are other religions besides Brahminism in India,—as Bouddhism, the sect called Djaïnas; and the followers of Nawik; and, finally, Mahomedanism. This last, the most numerous next to Brahmanism in India, is too well known to need any notice here, but of the three others it may perhaps be interesting to say a few words.

Bouddha is said to have been born in the North of India, of the family of *Sakya*—one of the most noble of the Brahmin caste. Many wonders attended his birth, and prophets called him the God of gods: his wisdom and beauty were superhuman, and the people were never weary of listening to him. Touched at the woes of the human race he withdrew to a desert, where he led so austere a life that his health suffered, and the milk of 500 cows was necessary to restore him. He then, at the request of the gods themselves, began to preach, overcame the five worshippers who opposed him, and spread his doctrines widely in India. They appear to be merely a reformation of Brahminism, from which Bouddhism differs principally in having a regular hierarchy, governed by a spiritual prince, in each country where it exists: it is sometimes a complete ecclesiastical empire—as, for instance, that of the Lamas of Thibet. The Brahmins violently opposed it, and between the third and seventh centuries of our era India was deluged with blood by the two sects, till at length the Bouddhists were driven from the country. Their creed however, prevails widely in Thibet, China, &c., and in the island of Ceylon. Some learned writers are much inclined to identify Bouddha with the early heresiarch Manes, who certainly took refuge in India during a portion of his career.

The sect of the Diaïnas appears also to be an attempt to bring back the religion of India to its original form; they reject with horror the Trimourti and all the fables connected with it, the worship of animals, and all the Brahminical superstitions. They believe in one Supreme Being, who is absorbed in the contemplation of his own perfections, and in no way interferes with this world; they believe matter to be eternal, and admit the metempsychosis, and the reward and punishment of men according to their actions, but without any intervention of the divinity. They never take food when the sun is below the horizon, and always have bells ringing, or gongs sounding, to prevent their ears being polluted with the words of passers by; they scrupulously clean their vegetables, lest they should destroy animal life. They have some well-endowed temples; one in the Mysore is in the centre of three mountains, on one of which is a colossal statue of the celebrated penitent Goumatta, 70 feet high, sculptured out of a single piece of rock.

The religion of Nanuk is professed by the Sikhs. They too reject the Trimourti, and worship one Supreme Being, to whom they address their prayers directly. Warriors by profession, they nevertheless cultivate the earth and keep flocks.

There are also a few Parsees, followers of Zoroaster, scattered through the country as merchants at Bombay, and here and there a few Jews, making perhaps about 100,000 in the whole of India. Were it possible in this short sketch to dwell at more length on this subject, it would be interesting to point out the extraordinary resemblances between Hindoo traditions and Scripture history; we find, disfigured by their wild idolatry, traces of the lives of Abraham, Moses, Job, Samson, and others, and several of the sacrifices have clearly been borrowed from the Jewish law. Some of their accounts of the creation and of the deluge strongly recal and almost repeat the words of the book of Genesis. They speak of the first man and woman being created innocent and falling into sin, also of an earthly paradise: the history of Chrishna, for instance, has a singular resemblance to that of Moses; but our space forbids us to pursue the parallel. The Hindoos are supposed to be descended from Shem, though it is probable that the race of Ham is mingled with them, and as Jews were certainly settled in India and China as early as three centuries before the Christian era, they might have borrowed much from them. We even find a distinct prophecy of an expected Saviour containing the very name of Jesus, and certainly more ancient than the coming of our

Lord. The great antiquity once attributed to Hindoo records, which carried them back far beyond the Mosaic era of the creation, has been distinctly disproved, and is now abandoned by all. Of the four yougarus, or periods, into which they divide their history, the three first are clearly fabulous, and are in fact so reckoned by themselves, as they date everything from the commencement of the fourth, or iron age, in which we now live; it goes back to the period of the deluge, and agrees wonderfully with our common chronology, the difference being only sixty years. Many writers whose acquaintance with this subject will not be questioned, declare that all the histories and antiquities of India confirm what is related in our Scriptures.

INTRODUCTION OF CHRISTIANITY INTO INDIA.

We find in the earliest Christian writers and traditions that the Apostle St. Thomas preached in India; on this point the testimony of St. Gregory Nazianzen, St. Jerome, Theodoret, and others is quite clear, and the traces of Christianity found by the Portuguese confirms the fact. Among others a plate of copper engraved with half obliterated letters was dug up in 1543, and presented to Alphonsus de Sousa, the Portuguese governor. A learned Jew deciphered it as a donation from a king to the Apostle St. Thomas of land on which to build a church. When the foundations of the fortress of Goa were being dug, they discovered ruins of an old building, and among them a bronze cross, with a figure of our Saviour fastened on it. And what is yet more curious, in 1568 some Portuguese at Meliapore, wishing to build a chapel on a hill near the tower, where tradition said the Apostle had been martyred by the Brahmins, they discovered in digging a white marble slab, 2 feet long by 1 ft. 6 wide, on which was carved in relief a cross, whose four points were flowers. It was surmounted by a dove, which seemed to peck at the top of the cross. Around it was a triple arch, and beyond that, strange characters. The cross and the stone were stained with blood. After some time a learned Brahmin was found who read the inscription in the following words:—"Since the Christian law appeared in the world, thirty years after the 21st of the month of December, the Apostle St. Thomas died at Maliapore where there was a knowledge of God, and a change of law, and the destruction of the devil. God was born of the Virgin Mary, was obedient to her for the space of 30 years, and was God eternal. This God taught His law to twelve apostles, and one of them came to Maliapore with his staff in his hand, and built a church there; and the Kings of Malabar, and of Coromandel, and of Pandi, and of several other nations, willingly resolved, agreeing together, to submit themselves to the law of St. Thomas, a holy and penitent man. The time came when St. Thomas died by the hands of a Brahmin, and made a cross with his blood." Another Brahmin from a distant country gave a similar translation of it, without concert with the first. All this was attested at the time, and sent to Portugal to Cardinal Henry, afterwards King. In 1521 a sepulchre was found at Meliapore, containing bones and the head of a lance, part of an iron-shod stick, and an earthen vessel; the traditions of the place left little doubt that these were relics of the holy apostle. We dwell on these facts principally because they confirm what we have said above of the traces of Judaism and Christianity in the religion of the Hindoos; if Jews were settled in India three centuries before our era, and if St. Thomas preached Christianity there, it is easy to see how disfigured portions of both might have been mingled with the religion of the country. Nothing is known of Christianity in Judea for a length of time after the preaching of the holy apostle, but it must have been widely spread by him, from the great extent of country in which are found persons boasting that their ancestors were his disciples. About the 9th century Nestorianism spread from Persia, where it was very prevalent, into India, and it exists there to this day.

After the settlement of the Portuguese in India, Goa was erected into an archbishopric, with several suffragan sees; but the progress of Christianity was very slight till the arrival of the great apostle of the Indies, St. Francis Xavier, one of the first associates of St. Ignatius, the founder of the Society of Jesus. He landed at Goa, May 6, 1542, and at once devoted himself to the reformation of the nominal

Christians whom he found there: for so addicted had the majority of the Portuguese become to the acquisition of worldly riches, that they wholly neglected the duties imposed by their faith; while if any poor idolater were convinced of the truth by the efforts of the few missionaries then in the country, he dared not embrace it for fear of the oppressions of the Pagans. St. Francis and his companions quickly changed the face of Goa; and having wonderfully revived religion there, they went to preach along the coast of the fisheries on the South-west extremity of the Peninsula, where the inhabitants were so oppressed by their Mahomedan masters that they had sought the help of the Portuguese, who came to their assistance; in gratitude for this aid they willingly listened to Christian preachers. Almost the whole nation was converted by the wonderful zeal of St. Francis; and short as was his stay, the seeds he sowed continue to fructify to this day, notwithstanding the scarcity of religious teachers, and the many other difficulties with which Christianity in India has had to struggle. St. Francis also preached on the Travancore coast, which extends about 30 leagues: in a short time it was almost entirely Christian, and 40 churches were built, surrounded by fervent congregations. Though deplorably neglected since, from many circumstances to be detailed hereafter, the majority of the inhabitants of this district are even now Christians. The career of St. Francis Xavier is too well known to every reader of the Saints' Lives, and to every one interested in the progress of Christianity among heathen nations, to require further mention here. It is enough to say, that finding so vast a field was open to him, and how readily the nations embraced the truth, he wrote repeatedly to Europe for more missionaries, and many joined him. Being Superior General of the Missions of India, he could dispose of all who came out as he saw best, and direct their energies to work out the good which he had begun with such astonishing success. He attached himself chiefly to those countries which listened readily to his teaching. Once when he was on the coast of the fisheries he disappeared into the interior of the country for a week, and on his return said that those people were not yet fit for the kingdom of God, nor was anything more ever known of his excursion into the

Madura district. At first there were none but Portuguese Missioners in India, but gradually Priests of other nations, and of various religious orders came forward, and the progress of the faith was very rapid. Among these Missioners were many Jesuits: in the reign of Louis XIV of France, as many as sixty French Jesuits were sent out: they spread themselves over most parts of India, and established several Missions, which flourished till the destruction of the Society.

The object of the present memoir is to speak of the Mission of Madura which was founded by F. Robert dei Nobili, nephew of the celebrated Cardinal Bellarmine. Born in 1577, in Tuscany, of a distinguished family, he entered among the Jesuits at Naples; and while still a novice, the historian Orlandini, his master, foretold that he would do much to promote the glory of God in India,—for which he offered himself as soon as he had completed his studies. On reaching Goa he was sent to the Malabar coast: whence he proceeded into the kingdom of Madura, where the king, an ally of the Portuguese, had allowed a Christian church to be built for the Paravas who resorted there for traffic. F. Gonsalvo Fernandez, a most fervent and zealous Missioner, had laboured there for fourteen years, but had not converted a single native of Madura. The contempt felt for the Portuguese in consequence of their eating beef, drinking wine, and communicating with Parias, made the people fear to degrade themselves if they embraced their religion. F. dei Nobili resolved to strike at the root of this obstacle: he said—"I will become as a Hindoo to save these Hindoos": following the example of St. Paul, and making himself all to all to win all to Christ. After several years of study and preparation, he, with his superior's permission, presented himself to the Brahmins, declaring, with strict truth, that he was not a Portuguese, or, as they called them, *Prangui*, but a Roman rajah—that is, a noble—and a Suniassi—that is, a penitent who has renounced the world and its enjoyments. The life to which he thus condemned himself was most severe: he could associate only with Brahmins; his whole food was milk, rice, herbs, and water, once in the day; his dress a long robe of yellowish cotton, covered with a surplice of the same; a white or red veil on his shoulders; a cylindrical cap on his head; and on his feet wooden soles resting on props two inches high, and held on by a peg passing between the great toe and the next. To this he added a cord, the distinctive mark of the Brahmin and Rajah castes, but theirs consists of three threads only, while his had three of gold and two of silver, and supported a cross. He told them that the three golden threads denoted the three persons of the Blessed Trinity; the two silver ones the body and soul of the adorable Human Nature of Christ; and the cross His Passion and death. He separated himself from F. Gonzales, and built a church and a house in the Brahmin quarter of the city, where he buried himself in prayer and solitude, never quitting his house, and allowing visits with great difficulty. Curiosity is a great stimulant; and to those who came to see him his disciple used to answer that he was praying, or studying, or meditating on the Divine law; and when admission was at length obtained, the Father was seen seated cross-legged, in Indian fashion, on a dais two feet high, covered with red cloth, and with a carpet and a fine mat before him. All saluted him by raising their joined hands above their heads, and bowing them to the ground; even the noblest did this; and those who wished to become his disciples repeated it three times, and then went and stood behind him.

His very extensive learning, the purity and perfection with which he spoke Tamul, and his extensive acquaintance with Hindoo poetry and literature, delighted everyone, and his fame spread widely. The king wished to see him, but as he did not think it yet time to appear in public, the reply was, that the Suniassi was absorbed in prayer and contemplation. It was taken for granted that he did not wish to go into the streets lest he should sully his eyes by looking on women: so high was the idea of his chastity: a virtue the more admired by the Hindoos because it is very little practised.

But this vain reputation was not F. dei Nobili's object, he aimed at the salvation of souls, and to succeed the better in this he bound himself by vow to follow this new and painful life till his death. His first conquest was a Gourou, or priest, with whom he disputed four or five hours a day for twenty days. An abstract of this discussion would be both curious and interesting, but only a short account can be here given of his wonderful and most successful labours.

Gradually disciples collected around him, and he instructed them in the Catechism, and tried them well before he granted them Baptism. Several among them were very remarkable for their holy lives, and Albert, the Gourou above named, had great power over evil spirits, and became distinguished for his sanctity. *Possession* * was common among the Hindoos, as may well be imagined from the lives they lead, and Albert cast out many demons, sometimes obliging them first to testify publicly to the truth of the doctrines preached by F. dei Nobili; which made a great impression on the heathens. The good Father himself was also gifted with the power of healing miraculously, and during the time that he considered it conducive to the conversion of the heathens to remain secluded, he several times sent his reliquary, by some of the converts, to sick persons, who were healed at its touch.

* To this day the visible action of the Evil Spirit is by no means uncommon in India, and what reason is there to disbelieve the present existence of what we know on the authority of Scripture to have unquestionably existed formerly? If Christianity has diminished the power of the devil in Christian countries, we may naturally suppose that his power remains unbroken where the cross has never been planted.

After a time his great success excited the terror of the Pagans and a persecution was raised against him, but he quietly continued his proceedings, availing himself of the protection of some powerful friends whom he had secured; and the storm passed away, as did others at different times. By degrees F. dei Nobili showed himself more in public, as he found he could venture to do so without shocking the prejudices of those whom he wished to gain to Christ. In one of his letters we find the following account of his day. 1st. The usual exercises of the Society: that is meditation, Holy Mass, self-examination, spiritual reading, Divine office, &c. 2nd. Study of the Sanscrit and Badage tongues, and of the Vedams, or Sacred Writings of the Hindoos. 3rd. Composition of a large Catechism suited to the people. 4th. Four instructions daily to Catechumens and to Christians. 5th. Audiences given to friends and to those curious to see him, in which he had to listen patiently to the most ridiculous tales. For forty-five years he led this life, converting immense numbers, and gradually associating other Missioners in his labours .At one time a ridiculous report reached Europe that he had turned Pagan, and his uncle, Cardinal Bellarmine, wrote him a long letter to remonstrate with him against such a crime, to which he replied by showing the great influence he had gained by his way of life, and giving a full account of his motives, which entirely satisfied his holy and learned uncle.

His reasons for thus adopting native customs, and mingling among the natives as one of themselves, have been much questioned not only by Protestants, but even by Catholics, apparently incapable of understanding the difficulties he had to contend with, or of appreciating his success. The contrast between the uselessness of all the efforts of his holy and zealous predecessor, F. Gonzales, and the numerous converts made by him and those who trod in his footsteps, ought alone to be a sufficient reply; but when it is added that the good thus done has not been effaced by the long years of spiritual destitution which followed the destruction of the Society of Jesus, and that he acted throughout with the permission of his Bishop, we think every cavil must be silenced. So clear and forcible was his explanation, that it had great weight in inducing Pope Gregory XV later on to allow the converted Brahmins to retain certain caste distinctions and customs, which though apparently superstitions, were by themselves looked upon merely as marks of their nobility. The indomitable pride of the Brahmins, which seems born with them and nurtured from their earliest breath, has always been a great bar to their conversion. The system followed by Father dei Nobili was the only method which ever met with success amongst them. Their dread of lowering themselves among their fellows by a change of religion, and being looked upon as Parias for associating with Europeans or Parias, was to most an insuperable barrier, which F. dei Nobili removed in a great measure by the manner of life which he led. This distinction of castes, and the contempt felt by the members of the higher castes for all beneath them, is still a great hindrance to the spread of Christianity; so much so that even Catechists have been known to object to instruct those of a caste inferior to their own, and when native Hindoos have been educated and ordained at Rome, those of a higher caste have found it difficult to acknowledge their sacred character.

Father dei Nobili and a few others laboured,

as we have described, for five and forty years. The Mission was supported entirely by the resources spared with extreme difficulty by the establishments in the province of Malabar; for as Madura did not belong to Portugal, it received no funds from that country. The strict poverty practised by the Missioners enabled four to subsist on a sum calculated for only two: one was maintained by a small pension from his family; and two others by the Rector of the College on the Fishery coast; and by a house at Goa, with a little occasional help from the General of the order. Had their resources been greater, could F. dei Nobili have carried out his plan of establishing a College for Brahmin converts, and have been seconded by a greater number of Missioners, perhaps Paganism might have been destroyed in Southern India. As it was, these hard-working Missioners converted and baptized fully 100,000 idolaters. At length, sinking beneath his toils and privations, and nearly blind, F. dei Nobili was recalled by his superiors, first, to Jaffnapatam, and then to Meliapore, where he lived five years longer, exerting what strength and sight he had left in composing and dictating books in the native tongue for the assistance of his fellow Missioners.

Throughout his career he had been particularly devout to the Blessed Virgin, under whose protection he placed his Mission. To spread this devotion among his converts, he composed Tamul verses in her praise. He died at Meliapore in 1656, aged 80.

The loss the Mission experienced in him was some years later compensated by the labours of F. John de Brito, a Portuguese Jesuit, son of a viceroy of Brazil, who chose the Madura Mission as the most laborious, and who toiled in it and in the neighbouring districts with almost incredible success. He may be called the founder of the Mission of Mysore, and is supposed to have brought nearly 60,000 Hindoos to the faith. He had made many converts in the province of Marava, when the prince Ranganadadeven forbad him under pain of death to remain in the country or to preach to his subjects. He withdrew for the time, intending to return very shortly, as he could not resolve to abandon his converts, and looked on martyrdom as a great happiness. He was however ordered by his superiors to go to Europe, as their Procurator-General, and he reached Lisbon in

1687. The king of Portugal endeavoured to detain him in Europe, but he replied that many were capable of filling the high posts offered him at home, but in Madura there were few Missioners, and even if many should be willing to go thither they had not the advantage of knowing the language and manners of the people as he did. On his return to Goa, he did not even wait to recover from a severe illness he had contracted on the voyage, but proceeded at once to all the Jesuit establishments in Madura, of which Mission he had been appointed visitor. He then went to Marava, where there were several churches scattered among the forests. The heathen priests soon put his life in such danger that he could not remain two days in one place without great risk; but the blessing granted by God to his labours in the baptism of 8000 converts supported and consoled him during the fifteen months which elapsed before his martyrdom. Prince Teriadeven, one of the principal lords of that country, which his ancestors had once ruled, was seized with a mortal disease, and reduced to extremity; finding no benefit from his false gods, he sent to beg F. de Brito either to come to him, or to send a catechist to teach him the doctrines of the Gospel; a catechist was sent, who repeated a portion of Scripture over him, and he was instantly cured. He again entreated F. de Brito to come to him, which the holy Missioner ventured to do, and celebrated with him the Feast of the Epiphany in company with 200 newly baptized converts His zeal, his powerful preaching, and the joy displayed by the new Christians, so struck Teriadeven that he begged to be baptized also, but F. de Brito told him he did not yet know the pure life required by Christianity, and that it would be a sin before God to baptize him till he was duly instructed and prepared. He then explained to him the Gospel law regarding marriage, which was very necessary, as Teriadeven had five wives and a multitude of concubines. He answered that this difficulty would soon be removed, and instantly went to his palace, summoned all his women, declared to them that he was resolved to spend the rest of his life in the service of so good and powerful a Master as the God of the Christians, and that as His law forbade more than one wife, the others should receive a suitable maintenance, but he must separate from them entirely. They tried to move him by prayers and tears, but he was firm. His youngest wife, who was a niece of Ranganadadeven, went to her uncle with bitter complaints, in which she was supported by the heathen priests, who had long hated F. de Brito because the number of his converts much lessened their income. They told the king that the greater part of the temples were abandoned, no sacrifices offered, no festivals held in them, and that they intended to withdraw from the kingdom, that they might not witness the vengeance which the offended gods would take on all who countenanced such wickedness. Ranganadadeven immediately ordered all the churches to be burned, all the houses of the Christians to be pillaged, and a heavy fine levied from all who persisted in this creed, which orders were so strictly obeyed that many Christians were completely ruined. On the 8th January, 1693, F. de Brito was seized, together with a Christian Brahmin named John, and two boys, who would not leave him. Exhausted in health by the hardships of the twenty years he had spent in Madura, he was so weak that he fell repeatedly, but was forced by blows to rise and walk on, though his feet were bleeding and greatly swollen. At one village they were exposed for a day and a half to the mockeries of the people, placed on one of the idol cars, and before they reached the court a catechist, to whom F. de Brito had given charge of one of the churches, was added to their number. Prince Teriadeven succeeded for a time in lessening the harshness with which they were treated, but notwithstanding his efforts, days passed in which no food was given them but a little milk, once in the twenty-four hours. He also tried to induce Ranganadadeven to make some of his leading Brahmins dispute publicly with F. de Brito, but was answered by a command instantly to worship some idols which were in the room. He refused, saying he had lately been healed of a severe illness by the holy Gospel, and could not renounce it to the destruction of both his soul and body. A young lord present, who had also been healed by F. de Brito, obeyed the king's command, and was instantly attacked again with his disease, so violently that he was soon at the point of death. He entreated to have a Crucifix brought him, and cast himself before it, begging God's pardon for his sin.

Hardly had he finished his prayer when he found himself quite well. Ranganadadeven next had recourse to magic arts, to compass F. de Brito's death by the power of the gods; but he thrice repeated ceremonies which were believed all over the country to be inevitably fatal to any one they were used against, and of course they had no effect on the holy Confessor. Another ceremonial, believed to be all-powerful over gods as well as men, was then tried, but equally in vain. Still the king and the Brahmins only repeated that F. de Brito was the most powerful enchanter ever seen, and they asked him if his Breviary, which had been taken from him, were not the source of his power, and whether it would save him from their muskets. They were just going to fire on him when Teriadeven threw himself among the soldiers, and said he would die too if they killed his beloved master. He was so much respected that Ranganadadeven dared not persevere, but sent F. de Brito secretly to his brother, who lived at Orejour, a distance of two days journey. His sufferings before he reached this town were frightful; for, as he was too weak to walk, he was literally dragged most of the way, and was fed on nothing but a little milk. Ouriardeven, the king's brother, first commanded him to heal him, for he was blind and paralytic; but F. de Brito replied that God alone could do this. He was kept in prison three days, almost without food, and at length was led to where a high post had been fixed in the ground. A great crowd soon collected. He was allowed time to pray in silence, and then he embraced and pardoned his executioners. They seized him, tore off his dress, and seeing his reliquary hanging by a string from his neck, and fancying it some charm, cut it off by a blow of the sword, which wounded him severely. They then tied a cord to his beard, fastening it round his waist, to bend his head forward, and were about to cut off his head when two Christians rushed forward, and threw themselves at his feet, protesting they would die with him; they were dragged away, and the holy Missioner's head struck off with a heavy hatchet, February 8th, 1693. To their astonishment, the body, though placed so as to bend forward, fell backward, and the almost severed head lay with the face upwards; they hastened to cut it off entirely, as well as his hands and feet; they then fastened the body to the post. The two Christians had their ears and noses cut off.

We have related the career and death of F. de Brito at some length, because his canonization is now under consideration. He is well remembered even yet in the country, and there is great devotion towards him and confidence in his power with Christ.

The next remarkable name which appears in the annals of the Mission is that of Father Bouchet, who was the founder and builder of the handsome church of Aöur, about 1690. Till his time the Missioners had in general concealed themselves as much as possible, living completely among the natives, and following their customs. Even with the greatest precautions they were afraid to enter any considerable village except by night. But F. Bouchet so endeared himself to the people that he thought he might venture to build a finer church than had yet been attempted, and to serve it more openly. The church of Aöur stands in a large courtyard, the inner walls of which are painted, and ornamented at equal distances by high pillars, on which rests a cornice surrounding the building. The altar is at the intersection of the cross, and eight tall columns support an imperial crown, its sole ornament. Gold and azure abound in the inside, and the whole architecture is a mixture of European and Indian, which produces a very good effect. The church is under the invocation of the Blessed Virgin, and was much frequented as a pilgrimage. It is still a place of great resort, but is one of the many churches founded by the Jesuits, and served by them till the suppression of the Society, which have since fallen into the hands of the Goa clergy, and are now held by them in defiance of the Vicars Apostolic, by a fictitious authority from the crown of Portugal: fictitious, because the power of Portugal never penetrated even for a moment into the interior of the country.

Experience, and the example of these fathers, proved that Missioners in the interior must practise the austerities displayed by the Hindoo penitents, and accordingly they dressed, as F. dei Nobili had first done, in a piece of yellow cotton, with wooden sandals; they lived on rice boiled in water, with a few tasteless vegetables, and sometimes a little milk; they drank nothing but water, often muddy and bad, and slept on the bare ground, or at most on a tiger-skin spread on boards. They lived in mud cabins thatched with straw, which in the rainy seasons were often very damp, and their whole furniture consisted of a few earthen vessels, with palm leaves for plates and dishes. God blessed their zeal: some of the princes granted them protection, and the people crowded to hear them and to be baptized. The fatigues they underwent, living on such bad food, are almost incredible. It was usual to prepare the Christians for each Confession as if they had never made one before, by repeating for them detailed acts of faith, hope, charity, and contrition, and the numbers of penitents were often so great that the Missioner could hardly find time to say his Breviary. Often troops of two and three hundred would come down, with their wives and children, having brought with them barely rice enough to support them on their journey, and allowed by their masters but a limited time of absence. The Missioner was frequently obliged to spend the whole night hearing the Confessions of the men, after having listened all day to the women, till, between want of sleep and want of proper food, he could hardly bring himself to eat when there was a moment to do so. The fervour of these poor Christians was most edifying; they would often travel two days' journey, or more, to receive the Sacraments, and attend some religious festival: many of them perhaps might fall short of provision before it was over, being very poor, and the richer ones would subscribe to purchase rice enough to enable them to reach their homes. The devotion displayed at these festivals was often most delightful to the Missioner, who saw by it that his sacrifice and labours had not been vain.

In the beginning of the last century the Jesuits had added to the Missions of Tanjore, Marava and Madura, that of the Carnatic, which extended nearly 200 leagues in length, and contained 16 flourishing congregations; there were also many Christians in Bengal, and in the dominions of the great Mogul. The French Mission of Pondicherry alone numbered fully 60,000 native Christians, and was increasing daily; and without counting the Northern districts there were at least 1,200,000 Christians in the Peninsula. Nor were these conversions ephemeral. The Missioners, treading in the footsteps of St.

Francis Xavier, spared neither time nor toil, and never baptized without ample preparation, and repeated entreaties on the part of the Neophytes. The innocent lives of the Christians, and their firmness under persecution, showed them worthy of the graces they received. The change of life produced by baptism was truly wonderful, and so astonished the heathens that they imagined the holy oils were some magic charm—so little could they comprehend such a complete alteration. Hereditary crimes were eradicated; converts from the robber castes ceased to steal; and Missioners have declared that they have heard the Confessions of whole villages of Christians without finding one individual guilty of a mortal sin. Their firmness under persecution was even more extraordinary, for the Hindoos are a cowardly people, and very accessible to flattery, but Christianity seemed to change their nature, and to inspire them with the most generous and heroic faith.

One instance of the fortitude displayed under persecution by a Christian convert is too remarkable to be omitted, though it was by no means a solitary case; but it is told in considerable detail in the letters of the Missioners.

Nilen Pilley was of the Vellala caste, and born a heathen. His penetrating mind and his good qualities won the esteem of all who knew him, and he was very religious in his own way. God, who intended to call him to a knowledge of the truth, tried him with heavy losses, which grieved him the more because he was married. He had formed a friendship with a French officer, named Benedict Eustache de Lanoy, who one day seeing him in very low spirits, spoke to him of the rapidity with which the goods of this world pass, and advised him to put his trust in the one true God, and he would find his melancholy vanish. Such conversations were frequently repeated, and the French officer explained the Christian faith to him. He reflected in the silence of night on all he learned, contrasting the perfections of the true God with the actions attributed to his false ones, and at length he told his friend he would become a Christian. Benedict de Lanoy sent him to F. Franzodi Buttari, an Italian Priest, who then had charge of that portion of the district. The Father, fearing that his Pagan relations, and the danger of losing his employment, might counteract his faith, deferred baptizing him, but the young convert so earnestly begged for it, protesting that, having once known the true God, he would rather lose fortune and life than abandon Him, that at length, after being taught all that was necessary, F. Franzodi baptized him under the name of Devasagayam, the Indian word for Lazarus.

He immediately endeavoured to win his friends and relations also to Christianity. He first tried his wife, who considered Christians as degraded, because all classes of them worshipped the same God. Devasagayam reminded her that the same sun gave light to the highest and to the lowest castes, the rain fell on all alike, and they all trod on the same earth. Gradually he converted her, in spite of the eager remonstrances of her mother, who assured her that if she became a Christian, no family of equal rank would marry her children. She was baptized under the name of Guanapou, which means, "spiritual flower." He converted several of his relations afterwards; and the Brahmins, who were very much incensed at his opposing their false gods, waited their opportunity of punishing him. Father Franzodi wished to build a church, and Devasagayam went to one of the principal Brahmins about the court, and begged him to ask the king for leave to cut wood for this purpose. The Brahmin replied by violent threats: to which Devasagayam only answered that he was ready to bear anything they chose to inflict, and returned home, praying earnestly that God would give him courage and constancy. The Brahmins easily obtained an order to have him put to death, and soldiers were sent to seize him. He had already sent word of his danger to his friend Captain Benedict Eustache, who came and persuaded the soldiers to delay a little: meanwhile a priest came, and heard Devasagayam's Confession, gave him the holy Communion, and exhorted him to be courageous. As he was taken away by the soldiers, several persons met him, and said he had degraded himself by becoming a Christian, but if he would adore the gods of his forefathers he might be restored to the king's favour. He replied that he valued no honours but those never-ending ones promised by the King of heaven and of earth to His faithful followers. When the king heard this, he ordered him to be ironed and closely confined. Benedict sent a friend to comfort him, which reached the king's ears, and he sent a message to the officer, desiring him not to meddle with what did not concern him. Devasagayam continued praying earnestly that Christ would, through the merits of His sacred Passion, enable him to suffer with courage.

Next day the king ordered him to be taken to a neighbouring forest, and there to have his head cut off; and that all who had become Christians should be persecuted. Some soldiers brought him word of the sentence, and he exclaimed: "I have long hoped for this happiness: your news is a source of great joy to me." On his way to the forest he was insulted by the country-people, but he answered cheerfully, and prayed as he went along.

A fresh order from the king commanded him to be cast again into prison, and he lamented the delay, fearing God did not think him worthy to suffer.

Soon afterwards the king commanded that he should be led from village to village mounted on a bull, and struck with rods: that when he was all over wounds he should be rubbed with pepper,—which should also be put into his eyes, nose and mouth; and that, when he was thirsty, he should have water from a cesspool to drink. This barbarous command was executed. Devasagayam repeated unceasingly the name of Jesus, and bore his ever-renewed torments so heroically, that the people cried out it was a miracle; yet many insulted him. One day his guards left him for a short time, and a Christian stole quietly up to him, and read him our Lord's Passion: when he came to the scourging at the pillar, Devasagayam stopped him, and shedding many tears exclaimed, that what he was enduring was not enough. Next day, as they were rubbing the pepper into his eyes, he said it was a good remedy for the sins committed by sight. Another day that the guards, either through pity or forgetfulness, omitted the pepper altogether, he reminded them of it, on which they tore his flesh again with blows, and left him in the hot sun, with only corrupted water to drink. He reflected on the gall our Saviour tasted, and swallowed it as if it had been perfectly pure.

He was then, by the king's command, kept in chains before the palace; but the Christians crowded to him to be healed of their diseases; and the king, enraged that a punishment he had inflicted to destroy Christianity, only made it more known, had him removed to a distance, and chained to a tree; where he was left without a roof to shelter him from sun or rain. His sufferings here were very great, but he was comforted and encouraged by a letter from Captain Benedict. After a time he was again removed, and a roof of palm leaves given him.

The executioner of this district had no children, and had vainly offered numberless sacrifices to his gods to obtain them: hearing that many were cured by Devasagayam's prayers, he spoke to him on the subject, and was assured that he would have a son, which accordingly happened not long afterwards.

The martyr wept continually for his past sins. He had a tender devotion to the Blessed Virgin and St. Joseph; so that they appeared to him in his sleep, and with them was our Lord, shining with light. Devasagayam awoke his companion, but the vision had disappeared, leaving only a brilliant light. The news of this vision spread about, and Christians and awakened heathens crowded to see him. The king, enraged to find that all he did to degrade him only made him more honoured, had him removed again, and commanded that he should be left to die of hunger; but those who came to see him brought him food secretly. He also had the happiness of again going to Confession and receiving the Holy Communion.

To terrify the Christians the king next commanded that they should be stripped of their property: many fled to another territory, and many, though grossly ill-used, remained firm in their faith. Devasagayam was accused as being the cause of their obstinacy, and would have been beheaded had not a Hindoo penitent, a great friend of the king's, represented that it was disgraceful to put a man to death for his religion; so his torments were renewed. One of the officers of his guard resolved to cut off his head; and the executioner who had obtained a son by his prayers warned him of it, and offered to help his escape. He wrote to consult Father Madrindram, the nearest Missioner, who replied that a soldier who had served his prince long would lose his reward if he were to fly at the moment of battle, and Devasagayam refused to escape, to the astonishment of the executioner. He was soon afterwards removed again, and once more chained to a tree, where he was left ten days without shelter. The Christians were forbidden to approach him, but the guards did not enforce the order.

Nearly three years had thus passed after his arrest, when the king gave a secret order for his execution. He learned it supernaturally, and took leave of his wife, begging that after his death she would go into another country, lest her relations should persuade her to apostatize, and promising that God would protect her if she were steadfast in her faith. He then made the sign of the cross over a sick girl who was brought to him, and healed her, and then prayed earnestly till the soldiers came to take him to a solitary place and shoot him. He told them he knew what they intended, at which they were much surprised. Finding he could not walk as fast as they wished, they made him lie down, and passing a stick through the irons that fastened his hands and feet, carried him, which was excessively painful, as the irons wounded his limbs. On reaching the spot he begged a few minutes to pray,—which was granted,—and then they fired three muskets at him; he fell severely wounded, exclaiming—"Jesus, save me"; and they fired again and killed him. They then withdrew, having taken off his irons and cast his body into a ditch. The Christians buried it in the Church at Cattar, and many were cured by the earth stained with his blood. He was put to death on the 14th January, 1752, seven years after his baptism.

The native Hindoo princes were not the only persecutors of the Holy Catholic faith: the Dutch settlers along the coast rivalled and even surpassed them in cruelty. On the Coast of the Fisheries a Dutch preacher wished to persuade a Parava chief that the faith he taught was superior to that the Paravas had received from their ancestors: the chief replied that he must prove it by working miracles at least equal or superior to those of the great Xavier; that he must raise a dozen dead to life, and heal all the sick. Force was then tried, but equally without success. Many endured scourges and tortures with the courage of the ancient martyrs, and their mothers rejoiced in their suffering thus for the sake of their Saviour. Children when threatened with death knelt down, and with clasped hands declared themselves glad to die for Christ. Many other converts suffered much from their heathen relatives, and were sometimes obliged to give up all they possessed, and carrying their children with them seek a subsistence in some other place; yet persecution, sickness and death, they cheerfully accepted from the hands of their merciful God, rather than abandon His holy law.

These flourishing Missions had often much to suffer, first from the internal wars among the native princes, in which their undisciplined troops scattered themselves over the country, and destroyed all before them, killing such of the inhabitants as had not hidden themselves in inaccessible places, and forcing the Missioner to seek a refuge on the sea coast, or in the mountains. On his return he often found his church burned, and his flock dispersed. All this became still worse when Europeans took part in these wars; the hatred they excited in those against whom they fought, and their conduct so opposed to their religion, weakened the effect of its holy doctrines and morality, and the more the Europeans became known, the greater was the prejudice against Christianity, as being the creed they professed but did not practise. This aversion became so violent that in some districts a heathen of good standing would not even venture to acknowledge an intimacy with Christians.

The controversy among the Missioners themselves regarding what were called the Malabar rites, was another circumstance which seriously checked the conversion of India. It is impossible for Europeans who have not lived in India to imagine the power of custom over the Hindoos; to them it is a supreme law, and all that goes against it is blamable and degrading. To oppose their customs would have been to alienate them entirely from Christianity, and most of the Missioners therefore tolerated all such as were not clearly forbidden by the law of God or of nature. Persons ignorant of the country attacked these concessions fiercely, and in their accusations mingled with the customs permitted by the Missioners to their neophytes many which they steadfastly opposed, as for instance the wearing of the *Taly*, a jewel engraved with an idolatrous figure, worn round the neck by married women in token of marriage, like the wedding ring in Europe.

In 1703 Cardinal de Tournon, Apostolic Legate in India and China, examined the question, and decided against the toleration of some of these customs; the Archbishop of Goa, the Bishop of St. Thomas, the Jesuit Missioners, and others, appealed from this decree to Rome. Pope Clement XI confirmed the decree temporarily, but appointed persons to examine the case more fully. It was long debated at Rome, and in 1727 Clement XII repeated the confirmation of Cardinal de Tournon's decree. However, it was found impossible to observe it practically. A fresh examination took place, and some modification of it was permitted in 1734, allowing for a time the omission of some of the ceremonies of Christening, the most offensive to Hindoo prejudice, such as the use of saliva, and the breathing in the child's face, recommending, but not obliging the Missioners to give the name of some Saint to those they baptized, and requiring them to observe, as far as possible, the regulations of the Council of Trent regarding marriages, which Hindoo custom would have celebrated in the childhood of the parties. Some of the festivals to which the Hindoos clung were prohibited, but others were allowed, and no penalties of censure were attached to this brief. The Missioners in general received it with joy, but some thought it did not sufficiently take native prejudices into consideration, and sent fresh petitions to Rome; however, in 1739 Pope Clement by a brief required from every Missioner in the country, or who should hereafter go thither, an oath of obedience to this decision, and it was cheerfully taken. Benedict XIV, his successor, published a bull containing a complete history of the discussion, confirming the brief of Clement XII, and ordering that any Missioner who would not obey it should be sent back to Europe. The Jesuits at once accepted this bull; they had always opposed the wearing the *taly*, and introduced instead a trinket engraved on each side with a cross, and fastened with a parti-coloured string of an indefinite number of threads, instead of the yellow cord of 108 threads worn by the heathens. To prevent superstitious customs at weddings, they obliged a catechist to attend them, accompanied by a Christian Brahmin, to see that our holy law was observed; but finding the horror of the Hindoos for the use of saliva and breathing, in the Christening ceremonies, they, with due sanction of the bishops, continued to dispense with them. The greatest difficulty was about the Parias. To have any intercourse with them, and especially to visit them in their huts, was to become an object of hatred to all other castes, who would not afterwards accept any service from a Missioner who had done so. After vainly endeavouring to overcome this prejudice, it was proposed to Benedict XIV that there should be a separate class of Missioners for these poor creatures, which was approved, and some of the Fathers at once devoted themselves to this painful duty, separating themselves entirely even from their brethren in the same country, and enduring all the privations imposed on this out-cast class. One Missioner would be seen moving about on horseback, or in a palanquin, eating rice dressed by Brahmins, and saluting no one as he went along; another, covered with rags, walked on foot, surrounded by beggars, and prostrated himself as his brother Missioner passed, covering his mouth, lest his breath should infect the teacher of the great.

This extraordinary measure succeeded for a

time, but it has now been entirely discontinued, as no longer essential. Sincere indeed must have been the honesty of purpose, and admirable the spirit of self-devotion which could prompt a man of education and rank to become thus the apostle of the outcast, and to cut himself off entirely from the only human consolation which remained to him in his exile—the sweet converse and company of his fellow-labourers and brothers in Christ. The outburst of long-suppressed love and affection in the earnest embrace of two early friends and near relatives who met privately after months of separation as Brahmin and Paria Missioner, is beautifully described in one of the early letters from the Missioners.

One of the most remarkable labourers in this painful Mission was F. Artaud, who has been called the Apostle of the Parias. He used to collect them in a courtyard near the church, and instruct them unweariedly; they would sit around cross-legged, and listen with eagerness; not a week passed in which he did not win seven or eight, and often a far greater number, to the fold of Christ. In 1748, it is estimated that there were at least 385,000 Christians in the eastern part of the Indian peninsula, and a greater number on the western side, besides several flourishing Missions in the north of Hindostan, whence the faith was rapidly spreading over all parts of the country. The island of Ceylon was so completely Christian when the Dutch took possession of it in 1650, that all their cruel persecutions could not eradicate it, though they actually sent to the main land for idolatrous priests to re-establish Buddhism, and prohibited the landing of any Catholic Missioner. Yet the faith was so rooted in the hearts of the people, that after 145 years of persecution it still lingered, like fire beneath ashes, to burst forth brilliantly when Priests could again appear.

CONSEQUENCES OF THE SUPPRESSION OF THE SOCIETY OF JESUS.

The source which principally supplied India with Missioners was suddenly to be dried up: in 1773 the Society of Jesus was suppressed by a brief of Clement XIV. The Malabar Mission was then entrusted to the Bishop of Tabraca and the Seminary of Paris. The Fathers of the society who were then on the Mission continued the good work they had begun, and deeply as they regretted their own superiors, they punctually obeyed those now assigned to them by Providence, looking on the new Missioners sent to Madura as beloved brothers and fellow-labourers. Most of the remaining Jesuits were old men, who had toiled for years among the natives, and were looked on by them with the greatest respect. Had we space, a sketch of their labours would be most interesting, but we must proceed with our narration. F. Mosac, the superior of the Mission, gave way at once to the Bishop of Tabraca, by whom he was superseded after forty years of labour, during which he had baptized above 40,000 persons, chiefly sick children. He lived but a short time longer, occupied in prayer and the exercises of an interior life. The new and the old Missioners worked on harmoniously, till the great French revolution destroyed the Seminary for foreign missions at Paris, and for many years afterwards the Christians of India were left with but very few Priests. In 1802 the French missions in that country had but fifteen European clergy besides the bishop, and most of these were old men, too weak to penetrate into the interior of the country. They were assisted by four native priests. The Mission was divided into ten districts, several of the more inland of which had but one Priest, who, though perpetually travelling from place to place, could scarcely visit each congregation of his scattered flock once in a year.

In 1817 there were but five or six aged European priests, and a Vicar Apostolic, in the whole of this Mission; there was a little college at Pondicherry, where from time to time a few native priests were ordained. A few years after, the establishment for Foreign Missions sent a few clergy out to this country, and in 1824 there were fifteen priests; but many of them were old, and had they been in the most vigorous health they could have done but little among so many Christians, scattered over such an immense extent of country. The Vicar Apostolic wrote most pressingly for a supply of Missioners, stating that there were congregations of 3 or 4,000 souls who saw a priest but once in two years, and that even those who had a Missioner living amongst them were very insufficiently attended: for what could one man do among 7 or 8,000 souls, scattered sometimes upwards of thirty-five miles apart?

In 1830 he had the grief of seeing some Christian families, who had been entrusted to the priests of a neighbouring district, from the impossibility of attending to them, and who had long vainly implored to have French or Jesuit Missioners sent to them, give themselves up to the Protestants. In 1836, Mgr. d'Halicarnasse, who had toiled for forty-seven years in this Mission, which he had governed as vicar apostolic for twenty-two years, got M. Bonnand, Bishop of Drusipare, appointed his coadjutor, and soon afterwards died. There were then but sixteen priests in the whole Mission of Pondicherry. The congregation of foreign missions, which has to supply five large countries in the east, found it so impossible to procure priests enough for Madura, that the proposal of the Propaganda to send Jesuits there again was gladly accepted. In 1837 four members of the society reached Pondicherry, and five more followed during the two subsequent years. Spread over the interior of the country, they at once endeavoured, under the guidance of Mgr. de Drusipare, to revive the old Christian congregations. By a brief of 1836 various vicariates were established in Asia, according to the wants of the different countries. The island of Ceylon was erected into a separate vicariate apostolic: Madura, Tanjore, Marava, and the Mysore, were committed to the charge of Mgr. Drusipare, as vicar apostolic of the Coromandel coast; the former dioceses of St. Thomas and Meliapore were annexed to the vicariate apostolic of Madras; the ancient dioceses of Cranganor and Cochin to that of Malabar; and authority over all these was given to the Vicar Apostolic of Verapoly; Malacca, and the country beyond the Ganges, were subjected to the vicariate apostolic of Ava and Pegu, and another vicariate was established at Bombay; Calcutta was also made a separate episcopal charge, and some few years later was made an archbishop's charge, Dr. Carew being raised to that dignity. To these we must add the Archbishop of Goa, formerly primate of the Indies, whose diocese has been narrowed to the small limit of the Portuguese possessions. These arrangements of the Holy See have been disputed by certain Portuguese and Indo-Portuguese priests, who, themselves unable to manage this immense country, cannot bear to see it transferred to other hands.

To understand the state of things in this respect, to explain the fatal opposition of Portugal and those influenced by her to the new arrangements of the Pope, to describe, in short, what is called the Goa schism, which has so miserably checked the progress of religion in India for many years past, it is necessary here to give a slight sketch of what may be called the political history of Christianity in India.

Among the Portuguese navigators who found their way to Hindostan by sea in the 15th century, were many knights of the Order of Christ, one of the military-religious orders instituted to fight against Mahomedanism. Many persons then thought that an attack made on those Eastern countries whence Islamism derived its strength, would, by creating a diversion, much benefit those who were endeavouring to drive it from Europe, and with this view these knights joined in the voyages of discovery set on foot by the Infant Don Henry of Portugal, their Grand-Master. To them, for the protection of Christianity, the first attributions of Indian territory were made by the Holy See, and not to the Portuguese king or nation. In those times the idea of taking possession of a newly discovered country by planting the national flag had not arisen, and all Europe considered the Pope as the arbitrator of differences, and as having supreme spiritual authority in the whole world. In the first grants made later on by successive Popes to the Portuguese crown of all the territory they might conquer in India, no mention whatever was made of the right of patronage, as it is called, which has been so fertile a source of some good, and of great evil. Portugal was however authorized to build churches and monasteries in the countries she conquered, and to send Missioners thither. Leo X was the first Pope who granted any right of patronage in these Eastern countries, but he attached to it, as a condition, that Christianity should be maintained and protected by the government; at the same time the right of advowson was limited to those districts of which Portugal then was, or might afterwards be, actually possessed. On these terms four bishoprics were, at different times, erected in Hindostan, and in 1557, Goa, the chief seat of Portuguese power, was erected into an archbishopric, to which the others were made suffragans. The kings of Portugal very soon tried to claim under these grants far more extensive rights than had been intended by the sovereign pontiffs, and Urban VIII refused to allow them any influence (as they claimed to have) over the nomination of bishops suffragan to Manilla, and also over the bishops and vicars apostolic sent to Japan in 1646, and afterwards to China. Portugal not only protested vehemently against this resistance to her aggressions, but ordered the governor of Macao, under pain of death, to let no one enter China who did not come from Portugal, and closed the African missions in the same manner. In this extremity, the power of nomination to the sees of Cranganor and Cochin was yielded to the king of Portugal, though both places were under Dutch rule. Alexander VIII extended the grant to the bishoprics of Pekin and Nankin in China; but it gave rise to such disorders that in 1696 Innocent XII dismembered these dioceses, to establish more solidly the authority of vicars apostolic; and the resistance of Portugal to the change was vain. As for the episcopal sees in India, they were placed under the patronage of this crown only on condition that they should be regularly endowed by the king in the districts he was master of; and the Holy See never gave up the right of modifying the limits of these dioceses, or making any necessary changes, whether they continued to be under Portuguese dominion or not, as we find in the brief issued by Clement X in 1673, *Solicitudo pastoralis*, and also in the words contained in the brief for the erection of each see, "*Jus patronatus ex meris fundationi et dotationi competere*"—"The right of patronage arises solely from patronage and endowment."

It is therefore evident that in reducing the extent of these ancient bishoprics, and even in suppressing them, the holy see has acted with uprightness and justice, while the resistance of Portugal has been unreasonable. This opposition has lost all shadow of *reason*, from the endowments granted by Portugal having completely ceased, so much so that in 1836 the vicar apostolic of Verapoly writes—"Since the change of government, the Court of Lisbon has ordered the magistrate last sent out to Goa not to give a farthing to ministers of the Gospel employed beyond the Portuguese territory; we may therefore feel assured that all pretension to the right of patronage over the sees of Cochin, Cranganor, and Meliapore, is abandoned." The same prelate adds—"For a long time there have been no Portuguese bishops at Goa, at Cranganor, at Cochin, or at Meliapore," and as Cardinal Fornari concludes, in accordance with most doctors of canon law, "When the cause for which the patronage was granted ceased, the right of patronage ceases also."

The Holy See, however, hesitated to exercise its undoubted right, and in 1832 Cardinal Pedicini, Prefect of the Propaganda, presented a request to the Portuguese Ambassador, that his Sovereign would either fulfil the obligations undertaken with regard to the Indian bishoprics, or would renounce pretensions which put a stop to all good in that country, and rendered ecclesiastical government impossible. He pointed out that Portugal now possessed nothing but Goa, and had in the rest of its former territories no claim but that of patronage, which it *could not exercise*. He therefore suggested that the Portuguese Sovereign should name a new Archbishop of Goa, and that the other Sees should in future be considered in the same position as the foreign Missions usually are. Still nothing was done till Gregory XVI determined to act decisively; and began by erecting, with the consent and approbation of the English Government, Vicariates Apostolic, at Calcutta, and at Madras, in 1834. Great opposition was made to this by Portugal, but the salvation of too many souls was at stake to allow any yielding on the part of Rome to claims so unreasonable. The Portuguese clergy seemed to have long acted on the principle, that it was better to let the people perish for want of religious aid than to see them receive it from *Turkish bishops*; so they called the vicars apostolic, whose titles were taken from extinct Sees in Turkey. They now called in the help of the secular power, and of the English Government, to check the execution of the Papal decrees. In 1836 the Sacred Congregation met to find means of remedying such abuses, and the celebrated Brief, *Multa Præclarè*, was carefully prepared, and meantime two more vicariates apostolic, at Ceylon and Madura, were created. The latter was not filled up just then, from certain circumstances, and its administration was temporarily committed to Mgr. Bonnand, Vicar Apostolic of the Coromandel coast. In 1838 a special decree annexed the old diocese of Meliapore to the Vicariate Apostolic of Madras, and those of Cranganore and Cochin to that of the Malabar coast, or of Verapoly. The Archbishopric of Goa had then been so long vacant, that the Portuguese clergy in India, having no one to recruit their numbers by fresh ordinations, were gradually becoming extinct, when unfortunately Portugal aroused from its long apathy, and pretending to enter into the views of the Holy See, demanded canonical institution of a new Archbishop of Goa, who, however, made a solemn promise to the Roman Legate at Lisbon, that he would submit to the arrangements of the Brief, *Multa Præclarè.* No sooner had he reached Hindostan than he broke his engagement, and confirmed all that the Goa clergy had done to oppose the new Vicars Apostolic of British India. He even went farther, and availing himself of some words inserted in his Bull of institution, to which he gave an explanation completely at variance with the intentions of the Holy See, he claimed all the rights of his predecessors, as Primate of India, notwithstanding a Brief which accompanied the Bull, and by which the Pope commanded him to respect the jurisdiction of the vicars apostolic.

He immediately ordained an immense number of clergy of all grades, taken from every rank of life; many of them quite uneducated, and but few in any degree competent for the ministry. This step ensured a long continuance of the nearly extinct schism caused by the previous opposition of the clergy of Portuguese origin to the establishment of the Vicars Apostolic. The archbishop also encouraged the intrusive Bishop-elect of Meliapore, nominated by Portugal, but rejected by Rome, and never consecrated; who, notwithstanding, proceeded to the visitation of his assumed diocese, and by so doing gave occasion to serious disturbances in many places. It is needless to point out the bad impression all this makes on the heathen portion of the Hindoos, or its still more deplorable effects on the Christians, who can hardly comprehend the point in question.

The impossibility of supplying European Priests in sufficient numbers, had gradually caused the missions in the South of India to lapse almost entirely into the hands of the now schismatic Goa clergy. They have possession of most of the ancient churches, to which the people are deeply attached, and where they prefer celebrating their festivals, and making their offerings, which, of course, cannot be permitted, as thus the schism would be supported.

The schismatic priests, unfortunately, spare no efforts to calumniate and misrepresent the legitimate Missioners, and to induce the people to keep them out of the churches. They win them over, in many cases, by giving the Sacrament of matrimony without requiring previous instruction, and by dispensing readily with the forbidden degrees of *affinity*, even it is said in some cases with the first.

In short, this unhappy schism is the great obstacle to all the efforts of Catholicity in India. Not only does it deprive our Missioners of the funds necessary for their support—funds which would even now be sufficient in many cases for the maintenance of religion—but it entails numberless expenses, which the poor native Christians are ill-able to bear, and which are an intolerable burden on the scanty resources of our missionary funds. Often new churches must be built, and in districts where there are tolerable ones already; and law suits must be carried on before the English tribunals, which amount to a heavy expense;

and would to heaven that expense and consequent privation were the worst evil entailed by the schism.

Happily the recent translation of Mgr. Torrer from the archbishopric of Goa to that of Braga in Portugal, to which, after much negotiation, his consent, and that of the Portuguese crown, have been obtained, has cut off the main spring of the schism, and in our sketch of the present state of the mission we will speak of the progress made in gaining over the poor Christians, and in some instances their misguided pastors.

SKETCH OF THE EFFORTS OF PROTESTANTISM IN SOUTHERN INDIA.

A short account of another class of missionaries in India may perhaps interest the reader. To us far less openly hostile than the schismatics, they are formidable as regards worldly means; obtaining, however, but little success among the people. These are the Protestants of various sects, who endeavour, with all the aid that wealth, and in some cases worldly learning, can give, to spread their different notions of Christianity among the Hindoos.

The first Protestant who ever landed in India was an Englishman, named Stevens, who came to Goa in a Portuguese ship in 1593, but he was a mere adventurer, without any political or religious object. Two years later the Dutch appeared in the Indian seas, established themselves in Java and Sumatra, drove the Portuguese out of the Malaccas, and by degrees conquered Cochin, and other important places on the Travancore coast, and at length the island of Ceylon, which they found almost entirely Catholic. Wherever they became masters they made war on the Catholic Church, not sparing the axe and the knife to enforce at least outward conformity with the confused mixture of Lutheranism and Calvinism, preached by their ministers. As before mentioned, they banished the Catholic Missioners, and prohibited their return under pain of death, which several underwent in reward of their endeavours to maintain the Faith among the people. Finding that Protestantism made no progress, the Dutch actually sent to the mainland for Buddhist priests, in order to re-establish in Ceylon idolatry which had been fast disappearing.

Numbers of the natives still remained Christians at heart, preserving a sort of traditionary recollection of Christian doctrines and practices, till, in 1815, the island fell into the hands of the English, when, on religion being set free, many loudly proclaimed their real belief. Ceylon has been divided into two new Vicariates Apostolic, and there are now again Catholic Missioners labouring among them, permitted by the English Government, though not assisted as the Protestants are. The Dutch have lost all their possessions on the Indian continent also, and therefore nothing further need be said of their endeavours to enforce their creed on the people: no trace remains of their efforts: the storm and they who raised it have alike disappeared, but Faith remains unbroken and unimpaired.

A few years after the Dutch invasion, the Danes tried, by more peaceful means, to plant Lutheranism at Tranquebar, and on several points of the coast. Their ministers shewed an eager spirit of proselytism, but as they were accompanied by their wives, and openly used spirituous liquors, in both respects going directly against the prejudices of the people, they made no progress among the natives, beyond spreading among the Catholics of Tanjore some of their calumnies against the true Church. In reply to these the learned Father Beschi, of all the missioners one of the most deeply skilled in the Eastern tongues, published in 1728 a controversial work which produced a strong impression on the native mind. The Lutheran mission at Tranquebar was in anything but a flourishing condition on the cession of the place by purchase to England a few years ago.

The foundation and gradual progress of the English East India Company in Hindostan is too well known to need an account of it here. For a length of time their wars with the French, the Dutch, and the native princes, occupied them too completely to leave time or funds for the propagation of their religion. An Anglican Bishopric was established first at Calcutta, and more recently, in 1834, by authority of King William IV, two others were established at Bombay and Madras.

In the beginning of the present century,

great numbers of ministers of various sects crowded to India, where there was no longer any risk of persecution. The Agents of the London Society of Missions appeared in 1806: they have fifteen stations, and spend nearly ten thousand a year in India. The Americans were also among the first. In 1810 the Unitarians arrived. In 1820 came the Wesleyans. In 1826 the Missionaries of the Society for the Propagation of the Gospel arrived: they spend about fifteen thousand a year. The Church Missionary Society has also its emissaries, spending at least ten thousand a year: and Baptist and Evangelical Missions have also been established. In 1836 the New Society for Indian Missions was set on foot: and the Methodists are also making immense efforts.

In many cities there are representatives of all these different creeds; for each of the above-named societies was instituted to remedy some error in the teaching of the rest. Their ministers are tolerably good friends on the whole, but attack each other's doctrines sharply, and this strikes the Indians the more forcibly, as their numbers are but few; and they frequently contrast the perfect agreement in the teaching of the Catholic missioners with the contradictions they hear from all the rest. It would be interesting to note the changes in doctrine which the various Protestant denominations in India have passed through, and now daily undergo. The alterations depicted in Bossuet's Variations, and more recently in Möhler's Symbolism, are surpassed here: the Reformation is unceasingly reforming itself, and would seem, in its effect on the native mind, to tend to the absence of all religion, or to pure Deism, as it has done in so many cases in Europe.

The distribution of numberless copies of the Sacred Scriptures in the native tongue was, of course, the first method of spreading Christianity adopted by Protestant ministers. It is needless to dwell here on the extreme difficulty of translating into Tamul a book such as the Bible, one in which a single word misinterpreted might often lead to the strangest errors. The unceasing disputes among the learned about the proper rendering of the sacred text into the languages of modern Europe, the many thousand faults stated, in the celebrated petition formerly presented to the king by the University of Oxford, to exist in the English authorized version, would be enough to convince any unprejudiced mind of the utter impossibility of doing justice to the Inspired Volume in a translation into Hindostanee by Europeans, however well versed in the Eastern tongues: so different are these in their genius from those familiar to the translators, and from the language in which the greater part of the New Testament at least was composed. The Tamul versions, got up with much pains by Protestant clergymen of unquestionable talent, are not indeed so strangely erroneous as those made into the languages of North America, or, to come somewhat nearer to the present day, those now printed in New Zealand, and in Otaheite, and in the Anglo-nigger dialect. But were they as perfect as human learning could make them, experience daily shows that the distribution of the Scriptures alone is not the way to convert heathen nations. The Apostles, who surely knew best how to spread the doctrines of their Divine Master, did so by preaching and oral instruction only. Armed with miraculous power, and an inspired command of the languages of those they addresssd, they could surely, had such been the will of God, have devised some means of disseminating the written word more easily than by the slow and expensive process of manual copying, and have left versions in all the different tongues of the globe to prevent mistranslation. Assuredly then, they did not consider individual reading of the Scriptures the way to bring the Gentile races within the fold of Christ. The fruitlessness of the Protestant missions, their failure almost everywhere to make even nominal Christians, and the sad condition of the morals of the people where Protestantism has gained an apparent footing, as in Otaheite, are undeniable proofs that the Catholic missioner, following in method as in doctrine the path trodden by the Apostles, has found the true secret of winning souls to Christ.

Independently of the millions of copies of Scripture scattered throughout India, the Protestants have distributed numberless tracts, some of them directed to disprove Hindooism and its many fables, and to teach the leading truths of Christianity. These are by far the best written, and are often really good. Some are controversial on the points in question between Catholics and Protestants. The Americans particularly have published many stories against Catholicity, turning into ridicule our religious ceremonies, and the veneration paid to the Blessed Virgin, to the Saints, and to holy images. These tracts are distributed by pedlars paid to go round the country for the purpose, and they are very clever in their business. Many of them were originally Catholics, who did not discover the *errors of Popery* till driven for obstinate misconduct from the bosom of her communion. Our Christians seldom take these books, but the idolators do, not however to read them: the cover is quickly torn off, the pictures cut out, and the printed pages make their way to the petty dealers. It is painful to Catholics to see portions of Scripture applied to such uses.

Many of the tracts distributed are clever, though they do not shew the same command over the Tamul possessed by the early Jesuits: frequently they translate the English idiom so literally as to be nearly or quite unintelligible to the natives. But were they never so well done, they could have little or no effect among a population of whom but very few can read, and where perhaps not one in ten of those who can will take the trouble to peruse the tracts placed in their hands. The sums spent in printing and distributing all these books are almost incredible; the Protestants themselves are obliged to acknowledge how few converts they have made, for in one of their tracts they say that perhaps not one copy in ten thousand is ever read, and of late years they have lessened the issue of them. Father St. Cyr, who has traversed the district of Madura in almost every direction, says that he never but once met a Hindoo who said he had been converted by reading; he was not then baptized, but had been promised a small pension by the Protestant missionary on declaring himself a Christian. This purchasing of converts is common among the Protestant ministers, and it is curious that it should not have won over more of the natives. The majority of their converts, except in Tinnevelly alone, were already Christians, and in Tanjore, Pratacendi, and Madura proper, they have gained many—some of these *by carefully assuring them that their religion was not in any degree different from that of St. Francis Xavier!* To maintain this delusion, they have in some places actually returned to

Catholic practices, which they had at first condemned, as for instance at Amapatty, where about fifteen families turned Protestant; the minister at first assured them that Confession was a modern innovation, but finding how much they clung to it, he yielded, and for a time heard the confessions of those who chose. In the same way the Sacrament of the Lord's Supper, as they call it, was at first administered by distributing pieces of bread dipped in wine, but after a time they, in some places, made the bread like the Hosts used by the Catholic clergy. Yet this imitation is by no means general; on the contrary, many of the Protestant ministers exhaust the usual topics of abuse and misrepresentation of Catholic doctrines and practices, and though confuted again and again, they persist in their assertions, as if they knew the realities of the Catholic creed better than those who profess it.

In many of the small stations their efforts are directed rather to make the Catholics become Protestants than to win the heathens to Christianity. Several of their schools are in Catholic villages; *their catechists are much more often sent to these, than to those inhabited by pagans*, nor, as has been already said, do they hesitate to give money as a motive for the desired change. The Hindoos are an imitative people, and readily follow any example set by their chiefs and by influential persons: a sum of money given, or a pension paid monthly to a few of these, will bring over many families besides their own; it is an almost irresistible argument with a native, and the only one that has much success in Protestantizing them. They will not give up the gorgeous ceremonies of idolatry for a sermon and a few prayers in a mean-looking church; they despise catechists whom they know to be well paid, and whose lives are by no means always calculated to win respect; and they turn their backs on married clergymen, who, say they, drink spirits, eat beef, and are served by Pariahs. But money is powerful, and if faith be not deeply rooted, or peculiar circumstances do not interfere, it is often convincing. This does not refer to money spent in supporting schools or catechists, but in some cases to actual cash paid down to purchase proselytes. Catholic Indians who had become Protestants—as the expression is, *for their bellies*—have gone to the Catholic missioner, and said that if he would give them a third part of the pension they were receiving from the Protestant minister they would return to the Catholic Church. His reply of course was, that Christians who would sell themselves were not worth buying. Were money less prodigally lavished, and motives of temporal interest no longer held out, Protestant missionaries in India would easily count their converts, whether from Catholicity or from heathenism. We do not wish to inveigh against Protestant missionaries. Are our own *always* irreproachable? Our business is merely to state a few facts.

Sometimes Catholics who have quarrelled with their Priest declare themselves Protestants, and this without an idea of the points of difference between the churches. Others have followed their chiefs, purchased as has just been said, and they *must* do so under pain of losing their daily bread. Indeed great numbers of those who call themselves Protestants remain so merely because, in their attendance at school, or in their dealings with Europeans, they have done things by which their caste was forfeited. But a few months ago, at a large meeting of the natives at Calcutta, the report of which appeared in the English papers, it was openly debated whether some means of regaining caste privileges might not be found, less burthensome than the almost impossible one of wandering for forty years as a penitent—the only mode now prescribed. It was added that the greater part of the so-called Christians employed by government, who are nearly all Protestants, would gladly return to heathenism if they could regain these beloved distinctions.

Money, however, is not the only means used to enlist worldly interest on the side of Protestantism. In several instances the ministers have bought lands, and it needs little acquaintance with India to know what immense power is possessed by the lord of the soil. This power has, on some occasions, been exerted relentlessly against all who do not become and continue Protestants—in name at least, for many of them are never baptized; often all that is required of them is to sign a paper declaring themselves members of the minister's congregation.

Another method sometimes used is rather startling. The minister engages that some cause then in dispute shall be favourably heard before the tribunals, provided the applicant will sign an engagement binding himself never to quit the Protestant religion, under penalty of from fifty to a hundred rupees. He then receives a recommendation, which is at all events popularly believed to assist his cause powerfully. The English government does not lend itself to this; indeed the use often made by some of the Protestant missionaries of the names of those in power in the country is perfectly unauthorized, and unsupported by facts, for there can hardly be, in any country, a body of magistrates among whom there is so high a principle of honour, or so much gentlemanly feeling as in the civil service in India. Rare exceptions may exist, and mistakes of course frequently occur, but they are attributable almost entirely to the great difficulty of coming at the truth through native subordinates, on whom *official reliance* must necessarily be placed. Instances often occur of native employés receiving money, but in the civil service of the present day this practice is entirely prevented by the high principle of honour which prevails. This does not prevent the existence of a general, one might say an instinctive feeling of hostility, on the part of the English government towards Catholicity, which is shewn distinctly in the fact that the government establishment for the orphans of soldiers at Madras is so completely in the hands of Protestants that it has been necessary in the case of Catholic orphans, to give up the great advantages of education it presents, and found by subscription an establishment wherein they can be maintained without sacrificing their faith.

Nor is this all. A Catholic named Claude Martin, a Frenchman of obscure birth, rose to be a general in the English service, and accumulated a very large fortune. He died in 1799, leaving, among other bequests, large sums to found schools in his native city of Lyons in France, and at Calcutta and Lucknow in India. He did not expressly stipulate about the religious teaching in these schools, but evidently intended them to be open to all. Were there an intention to exclude any, the donor, being a Catholic, would have excluded Protestants rather than Catholics. Nevertheless, regulations have been introduced which absolutely close these schools against the co-religionists of their founder!

The most effectual effort made by Protestantism in India, is the establishment of schools. The Hindoos are perfectly aware of the great value of learning, and will send their children wherever it may be obtained. Those of high caste are usually careful not to forfeit their rank by infringing on their peculiar customs; though, as has been said, numbers of nominal Protestants call themselves so only because they were considered degraded as Hindoos. The American missionaries at one time insisted on all their pupils eating beef cooked by a Pariah, the greatest degradation they could devise; and of course few but Pariahs would attend. But in most schools no pains are taken to Christianize the children beyond using the Bible as a school-book, (which by no means increases reverence or love for the Sacred Volume), and making them attend Protestant sermons, by depriving those who do not of some pecuniary advantages. They are not baptized, and comparatively few Hindoos, on leaving school, continue even nominally Protestant. Many of their scholars are the children of Catholic parents, forced to risk their religion by the sad want of Catholic schools. Of course numbers of these are perverted, or at least become indifferent to all religion; others, on mixing again among their families, return to the true faith.

Far more is done, we repeat, to win over Catholic children than those of heathens: all the usual falsehoods and mis-statements regarding Catholicity abound in the sermons of the ministers to them.* The boys who show talent are trained as catechists, and are, as such, secure of a comfortable maintenance. The difficulty of finding Protestant wives for these and other *employés* of the missions induced the ministers, seven years ago, to open schools for native girls, which deeply shocked Hindoo prejudices. None but Pariahs could be induced to attend, and even these were usually orphans. In some cases boys and girls beyond the age of childhood were made to attend the same schools, and the consequence was often such immorality as cannot be detailed.

The large funds supplied to the various Protestant missions enable them to maintain schools almost innumerable, and of all sorts: day-

* A little more than a year ago a public competition was opened at Calcutta for a considerable sum of money to be given to the native who could produce the best paper proving—"The Identity of Romanism and Heathenism!!"

schools, boarding-schools, and schools where board, lodging and clothes, are supplied to the pupils. It is impossible that such efforts among the young should not have considerable effect, at least in winning away those who, being already Catholics, though deprived of instruction by the poverty of the Mission, have not the prejudices of the heathen Hindoos to overcome. Had the Catholics means to establish anything like a sufficient number of schools they would not only meet the wants of their own flocks, but have their schools crowded with heathens who would grow up Christians, being baptized as soon as they were sufficiently instructed. Necessity alone drives the unhappy Catholics to risk their faith by attending other schools than their own.

Another mode was attempted at Palamcottah and Tinnevelly, where the ministers got possession of a district, and formed a sort of settlement, in imitation of the well-known Reductions of Paraguay. All the Hindoos living within this territory, about five thousand in number, were obliged to destroy their temples and idols, and give in their names as Christian converts, but they were not required to receive Baptism. It is said, that the greater part of them returned to heathen practices in a very short time.

The incomes of the Protestant ministers are very considerable. The salaries of those paid by Government vary in general from 300 to 700 rupees, that is, from about £30 to £70 per month. Those who are supported by the various missionary societies have usually 200 rupees, £20 a month if they are unmarried, and 250 rupees, £25 a month if married.

In the preceding pages many strong assertions have been made: names and instances could easily be given, but have been purposely avoided as invidious, it being the wish of the writer to express what has been his own impression on this subject—an impression formed by four years' residence in the country, and constant intercourse with clergymen of high position, both by birth and education, who have repeatedly been told by the natives what is here advanced, and in so many and such various ways, that it is impossible to withhold all credence. What has been said, moreover, will be in a great measure borne out by the following pages. It is by no means the intention of the writer to assert, that all the Protestant missionaries are self-seeking, and not in earnest in their work: instances of real and conscientious self-devotion are to be found, but the general system pursued is certainly not such as to command respect, or to convince those who behold their work, that they are the followers of the Apostles.

We have described the difficulties encountered by the early Catholic Missioners in India, and the self-sacrifice which led to their success. So much has intercourse with Europeans lessened the bitterness of native prejudice, that some of the most formidable of these difficulties are now smoothed away. But this is not the most striking point of contrast, between the career of the first Catholic and that of the modern Protestant preachers. The latter are supported by all the influence of a Government whose sway extends from sea to sea, from the snowy mountains of Nepaul to the tropical island of Ceylon: a sway respected by the people for its justice, and considered by the passive Hindoos all but irresistible. The sums of money the ministers have spent within the last thirty years cannot be rated at less than 200 lakhs of rupees, or about £2,000,000 sterling, and yet their own organs do not show more than 32,000 native converts from heathenism, being at the rate of at least £ 60 a head.

Catholics are not aware of the immense sums contributed by Protestants to their missions. In a condensed Report of the British and Foreign Bible Society we find that, since their establishment in 1804, they have expended £ 3,751,555, and that in 1850 alone they spent £ 103,330. This is but one of many societies employed in spreading their various and varying doctrines all over the world. We have not at hand the means of ascertaining how much of this large sum was given to the portion of India with which we are principally concerned, nor have we details of the money spent there by any Protestant missions later than 1848; but in that year we find, in the Report of the Madras Committee of the Society for the Propagation of the Gospel in Foreign parts, that they paid 170,000 rupees, or about £ 17,000, of which 50,197 rupees went for missionaries' salaries, 21,965 rupees for catechists and readers' salaries, 39,410 rupees for schools and seminaries, besides 1,379 rupees for school buildings. In the same year the Propagation of the Gospel Society spent

150,000 rupees; the Church Missionary Society 100,000 rupees; and 280,000 rupees were paid by Government to Protestant chaplains, all in the Madras Presidency. The German Evangelical Mission of Canara, during the year 1848-1849, states its expenditure at 48,354 rupees, of which 20,715 rupees were for the support of "24 brethren and 15 sisters" (the missionaries and their wives), 8,874 rupees for schools, and 2,118 rupees for catechists. Their Canarese school is attended by only 190 scholars, only 13 of whom are said to be Protestants, nor is it stated that these are baptized. These missionaries boast that they are not required to subscribe to any definite articles of faith, and some of them denounce the members of the Church of England, yet 11,175 rupees of the above sum were contributed by Englishmen. They report only three converts in the year: but no wonder they make so few, for they are busily purchasing land, and lending out money at high interest, sometimes receiving double the legal rate.

We have mentioned that much of the missionary expenditure is in printing and distributing tracts, and the degree of benefit thus produced we have briefly pointed out; but a few details taken from their own reports may prove on how large a scale they carry on this mode of conversion, if such it can be called. In 1848 the Madras Tract and Book Society distributed, in round numbers, 71,000 tracts, at a cost of 8,900 rupees. In the 31 years of its existence it has disseminated 2,950,000 tracts, at an expense of 370,000 rupees. The Madras Auxiliary Bible Society has circulated 550,000 Bibles, or copies of select portions of Scripture, at an outlay of above 500,000 rupees.

The Rev. G. U. Pope, in his report for 1846, speaks of applications made to him for books in a newly visited district as a most encouraging sign: the value attached to them, in very many cases, is in reality no more than the curiosity of so new a possession, and the use of them as waste paper. Not long ago a Catholic priest travelling through the country saw a boy flying a kite; it fell in the dust, and got dirtied and torn, but the child merely said, "Oh, we will go to the Padre and get another book." Some of those who had been long under instruction by the Protestant missionaries, on hearing the preaching of Catholic Priests and seeing the Crucifix which has ever been so valuable in illustrating and impressing the holy law of Christ, have declared that they have understood more in a few moments than they had learned from all the Bibles and Bible lectures of the Protestant teachers. This is not meant to imply that Catholics do not respect and value the Bible, but only that we do not consider the mere reading of it an infallible method of converting heathens, or that from it the uneducated are likely to learn their religion. To the Catholic church is due the preservation of the sacred volume amid the inroads of barbarous nations; she always encouraged its due use by the laity, and translations of it appeared in various European languages long before the so-called Reformation. Venerable Bede, who died A. D. 735, had translated it into Saxon, the language of England at that period; and in 1290 another version was made into the English then spoken. It had appeared in French before Luther began to preach, and was printed in Bohemian, in Flemish, in Italian, and in Spanish, half a century before he was born. The Spanish translation had been completed and circulated by St. Vincent Ferrer and his brother, with the sanction of the Inquisition; while a Castilian version had been made in 1284. German translations of the Bible were so numerous, and began so early, that it is said a history of the German language might be traced from them, the first being in 350, into the Gothic, from which modern German has sprung. During the seventy years that preceded the Reformation, while the art of printing was still in its infancy, and very expensive, upwards of seventy editions of the Bible were printed in Italy, Germany, France, Holland, Spain and Bohemia. No trouble was spared to make these versions accurate, and they would present a most favourable contrast not only with the strange translations made in modern days, by Protestant missionaries, into scarcely known heathen tongues, but even with the versions issued by authority in England, of which the one called Cranmer's Bible, which every parish church was forced to possess, was said in a subsequent royal mandate to be "disfigured with unfaithful renderings," some of which were corrected in King James's Bible, the present authorized version, though learned Protestants of all shades of opinion have admitted again and again that it still contains many important errors, and that a further revision is desirable.

But the greater part of the few converts the ministers claim, are, as we have stated, unbaptized, and are held to their nominal profession of Christianity only by gifts of land and money. In a Protestant periodical, *The Circulator*, for Dec. 19th, 1849, we find a letter complaining bitterly of the converts at Tanjore. Swartz, one of the early founders of this mission, had great influence with the Rajah, and was enabled to give to each of his neophytes a piece of land rent free for a time; supposing them now firm in the faith, Mr. Guest, the present missionary, endeavoured to obtain some small rent, but the converts rebelled immediately, complaining that he was depriving them of "privileges and immunities coeval with their first reception of Christianity." The correspondent goes on to say, that "They originally flocked round the missionaries to satiate their bellies with the good things of the mission, and they wish still to prey upon its vitals, and while the few who held situations of emolument grudge, with all the grudging of the most contemptible niggard, to give one rupee for missionary purposes, they squander large sums on night orgies, dancing girls, Brahmins, &c. The report of this same mission in 1823, says, there is great immorality. A great many have adopted heathen customs; many had fallen into the practice of polygamy."

The numbers of converts in this mission were estimated by Bishop Heber once at 40,000, in another place at 15,000 souls, yet he found but fifty-seven communicants, and but fifty for confirmation, though he was the first bishop who ever visited them. In 1847 Mr. Guest, with the help of six native catechists, and seven masters and mistresses, had but 970 baptized persons.

At Tinnevelly, the Rev. Mr. Pope reports, in 1849, that the numbers who had left his congregation were very large indeed, and this because he required them to send their children to school, not to intermarry with heathens, and to attend a Sunday school. In 1848 the Rev. S. Habbs, at the Sathhankullan district in Tinnevelly, complains of the continued and very considerable reduction of his flock, which he estimates at one-fifth of the whole, adding that "great numbers of those who have embraced Christianity in this province have done so without any strong conviction of its possessing claims to their belief very superior to those of their old superstitions: and they were received under instruction, simply in the hope that such a conviction would supervene."

The Rev. Mr. Newman, in his report on the Palamcottah district of Tinnevelly for 1848, after enumerating churches and schools built, Bibles distributed, and Bible-readings, says he doubts whether true knowledge of Christianity is on the increase, adding that "several of whom he had thought well, yielded up their Christian profession and departed from this world, after having long professed faith in Christ, with a heathen mark upon their foreheads and the name of a false god upon their lips." Another Tinnevelly missionary speaks of 104 back-sliders, of whom thirty-three were baptized and eleven communicants. This, by the bye, shews that unbaptized natives are reckoned as converts. In another instance a Rev. Mr. Bilderbeck reports that he preached at Ferampore to *a large, crowded, and respectable congregation:* the entry in his journal of that day says, "There were few persons inside; but about thirty persons stood out near the entrance door, who were passers by."

The Teloogoo Missionaries of Masulipatam, with more accuracy, report: "Our Teloogoo congregation properly consists of only two members, though four more, from their being connected with either our girls' school or one of the members, attend our Teloogoo services. But besides these six baptized persons, there are present at our Sabbath services all our heathen girls, about thirty or forty of the boys from our vernacular school, and most of our heathen domestics, so that we frequently have a congregation of about eighty souls."

The Rev. E. Sargent, writing from the Tinnevelly district on the 30th June, reports the backsliding of two villages. He says of some of his adherents: "their profession of Christianity is not influenced by any higher motives than that of having so long identified themselves with the *Vedan* (the Protestant religion) they are now ashamed to renounce it."

The Rev. P. P. Schaffter, writing from the same Tinnevelly district in June 1849, tells us that several hundred individuals of the Kurnvankolie congregation had renounced the profession of the Christian religion, and that the congregation "of Alankolum, having got back their lands from the Brahmins, and being now independent of the missionaries, shew a great predilection for heathenish practices and ceremonies." This requires some explanation: in several districts the heathen heads of villages, and others in authority, had grievously oppressed the poorer people, who found that by attaching themselves to the Protestant missions they were protected, and this so unhesitatingly that they became oppressors in their turn, to such an extent as to rouse the Pagans against them; and bloodshed ensued. This was the history of the well-known riots at Tinnevelly a few years ago. The details would be too voluminous for our space; suffice it to mention that the magistrates more than once expressed their surprise at the disturbances in so many Missionary villages, and said that the more Protestant natives there were in a place, the more police they required. This affair has by no means tended to attach the Hindoos to Protestantism, as the outrages committed by the proselytes, and defended by the missionaries, were most gross and notorious, and the consequent reprisals of the Heathens were dreadful. The so-called Christians disgraced themselves on the trials which followed these riots by their perjury and conspiracy. Mr. Douglas, the Judge, says in 1846, "The records of the trials themselves, as well as the experience of every judicial officer who has been in the Zillah, will affirm that the time and labour required to unravel a single Tinnevelly case would suffice for the disposal of two or three cases in almost every other Zillah." Mr. E. B. Thomas, the Collector, speaks of false accusations and conspiracy being rife, of "the adroitness with which evidence is got together in support of crime," alluding to cases in which Protestant Christians were prosecutors, and Heathens defendants; and from these circumstances Mr. Lewin could not help calling attention to the fact of this district abounding beyond others in missionaries. These are the Christians whom Dr. Spencer, the Protestant Bishop of Madras, held up at Bath in February 1848 as so superior to the Catholic converts, who in his opinion "have but exchanged one species of idolatry for another," who were, he asserts, well acquainted with St. Anthony, St. Francis, and the Virgin Mary, but scarcely one had heard of the name of Jesus Christ. Catholics in England are so accustomed to the credulity with which their countrymen receive statements against them, that they scarcely wonder at such a charge being made, though some may be surprised at a man who should be a gentleman and a man of truth and honour, stating such falsehoods; whether he knew them to be such or not, we leave to his own conscience, but had it been possible to have placed any one of the Tinnevelly Christians and a good Catholic native before the meeting, the Priests so calumniated would willingly have abided the verdict of even so prejudiced an assembly.

These few instances are quoted merely to shew how immense is the sum lavished on whatever seems likely to contribute to the spread of Protestantism, and to prove that, if their success has not been equal to that of the followers of St. Francis Xavier, it has not been because they are less favourably circumstanced.

The advantages given to Protestants by Government are numberless. The salary of the few Catholic Chaplains allowed hardly ever exceeds 100 rupees per month, or £120 a year;

more frequently it is only half that sum, and even less, though they have charge of all the Catholic soldiers, who in some regiments are as numerous as the Protestants. Before 1830 there were hardly any European Priests in India, and the 50 rupees per month, the usual allowance to Catholic clergy for attending the troops at a military station, was not very insufficient for men who were of the class of the great majority of the Goa clergy, and who had other means of support; nor was it very disproportionate to the work they did. But now almost all the Priests in India are educated Europeans, and are surely entitled to a support becoming their station, and the far greater attention they pay to their flocks. They cannot live as cheaply as a native, nor is it desirable that they should: in fact no one doubts the influence that social rank and easy circumstances have in securing respect from the uneducated; nor, wonderful as is the self-devotion of the Catholic Priesthood in countless instances, can it be expected that a sufficient number can be constantly found to supply the wants of our large European force in India, unless some of the comforts of life are secured to them in return for their indispensable labours. Protestant Chaplains are, as we will shew, highly paid. But are the services of the Catholic soldier less valuable than those of his Protestant comrade? are his wishes, his feelings, less to be considered? They are in truth stronger towards his Priest than those entertained by Protestants for their clergy; disrespect to a Priest irritates the Catholic soldier, and much ill-feeling has often been caused by the non-recognized position of Catholic Chaplains. A Protestant Chaplain has what is called military protection; an insult to him would be punished as a military offence; the sentries are obliged to salute him as he passes on duty, and he has access whenever he pleases to barracks, hospitals, and soldiers' schools. Nothing of all this is granted to the Catholic Chaplain; in some cases the right feeling of the Colonel supplies, to some extent, the omission of regulations, but it depends on his individual good will. A sentry is not bound to salute a Priest, even when passing on official duty, and this often creates ill-feeling among the men, for a Catholic soldier salutes as a matter of course, which his Protestant comrade probably will not. Two soldiers walking together off duty, have met a Priest; one, being a Catholic, salutes him; the other, a Protestant, does not, and on being asked by his comrade refuses: the Catholic has been seen to walk away, angry, knowing that if the Protestant Chaplain had passed, he (the Catholic) *must* have saluted him. Trifle as this may appear, it shews the tendency of the marked distinction so unwisely made. Nor is this the worst: there are many Catholic Chaplains in India not paid at all by Government. Some of the large, and all the small military stations are dependent on the unpaid services of any Priest who may chance to be in the neighbourhood, and whose time is already more than occupied with his own flock. Even when there are a considerable number of Catholics at a station, the authorities have often refused to grant any allowance for a Priest. Some time ago, at Mhow, in the Madras Presidency, the Catholics applied to the Bishop for a Chaplain, if possible a British one, and the Rev. Mr. Birch was appointed; but though the soldiers and their families, with the native Christians attached to the station, numbered three hundred souls, Government refused him any salary, while the Protestant Chaplain, whose flock did not amount to a hundred individuals, received the usual sum allotted to his rank. At Palamcottah, in the Madura district, the Catholic artillery men are seldom less than from twenty to thirty, and no Catholic Chaplain is paid. At Wuzeerabad, where there is a large number of soldiers, no salary is allowed for a Priest. But these are only a few instances, out of many, in which the Catholic soldier is virtually taxed, by being obliged to support, out of his small pay, the Priest whose services are as necessary to his good conduct as they are to his happiness here and hereafter. The Catholic Chaplains have no grant for travelling expenses, nor any retiring pension, whatever may have been the length of their service. The Protestant Chaplains maintained by Government amount to twenty-nine; of these, nine receive 700 rupees per month, or £840 per annum; the rest have 500 rupees per month, or £600 a year. They have besides 200 rupees per month allowances, when on their journeys to visit out-stations at fixed periods, and if they leave India after seven years' service, have the half-pay of a Major, £173 : 7 : 6 a year; if they serve ten years, their retiring pension increases to the half-pay of a Lieutenant-Colonel, £200 : 15; if they remain eighteen years, three of which may have been furlough, they have on retiring the full pay of a Lieutenant-Colonel, £ 365 a year. Should they be unable to serve seven years, the shortest period which entitles to these retiring pensions, they may be admitted to the benefit of what is called Lord Clive's fund, from which they will receive £ 63 : 17 : 6, and their widows half as much. The widows of Chaplains who have served seven years may receive, from the same fund, the pension allowed to a Captain's widow, and if the husband's service has been fifteen years, that allotted to a Major's widow. A Chaplain absent from India on furlough, after seven years' residence, receives £ 191 : 12 : 6 per annum, and if obliged by illness to return to Europe before the seven years, £ 127 : 15 per annum. Besides these liberal salaries, they receive considerable fees for marriages, registries of Baptism, and funerals, except in the cases of the military.

It is well known that there are many Catholic soldiers in the English service; in some regiments there are nearly as many as there are Protestants, and no one has ever ventured to hint that they are less brave, or have shrunk from sacrificing their lives for their country; yet their orphan children are systematically excluded from the asylums provided for the orphans of soldiers, by regulations which would ensure the sacrifice of their religion if they were placed there. Remonstrance has been vain: we have stated elsewhere how the institution called the Martinière at Calcutta has been so managed as to exclude the co-religionists of its founder. At Madras and Bombay Catholic orphans are virtually excluded from all Government establishments, and after vain efforts to induce Government to alter such rules as interfered with the faith of the children, the Vicar Apostolic of Madras has been forced to establish and maintain an orphanage for the children of Catholic soldiers, for which all aid from public funds has been refused.

The difficulties placed in the way of Catholic Priests, who wish to instruct the Catholic children in regimental schools, is another grievance: there are certain regulations on the subject, but they are often evaded, and practically the permission may be said to rest with the Commanding Officer. In 1849 the Right Rev. Dr. Hartman, Vicar Apostolic at Patna, visited Benares, a military station in his district, where there was no provision for a Priest. He found there were quite as many Catholic as Protestant children in the schools, but that they were utterly ignorant of the Catechism. He wrote to the officer who had control over the school, requesting that the Catholic children might learn their catechism at the same hour as the Protestant children did, which was the more easy as one of the masters was a Catholic: the officer granted the leave, but after a short time the parents complained to the Bishop that it had been withdrawn. He remonstrated in writing, and received a reply enclosing a letter from the Protestant Chaplain, stating that *as no other party was appointed by Government* to undertake any portion of this work, he considered it not only his duty but also his privilege to exercise an entire control over the religious instruction imparted in the artillery school; and he considered the introduction of a catechism unsanctioned by him was, on the part of the schoolmaster, an infringement on his authority; he added, that the interposition of a Vicar Apostolic residing at a distant station was an encroachment on his just privileges. Some time afterwards the Catholic Priest at Chunar was recognized by Government as appointed to visit Benares once a month. Surely the children of Catholic soldiers are entitled to the superintendence of their own Pastor, and to instruction in the creed of their parents, or else a man in becoming a soldier legally forfeits one of the dearest of privileges, is debarred from fulfilling one of his strictest duties, that of leading to God the children whom God has entrusted him with. The commanding officers of two regiments, successively stationed at Trichinopoly, positively refused the verbal and written demands of the Catholic Chaplain for leave to superintend the religious instruction of the Catholic children within the regimental school. These are mentioned as instances of the spirit which prevails throughout India, and of the impossibility of uniform justice without proper regulations duly enforced. They show that Catholic Chaplains, though receiving what may be called an apology for pay from Government, are but half-recognized: yet attempts are often made to interfere with them in the performance of their duties. Lately a nominally Catholic soldier died at Trichinopoly, but as he was, from his neglect of religious duties, out of the Church, the Chaplain refused to perform over him the solemn burial service of the Catholic Church: a friendly officer came to the Priest and warned him that he might get into difficulties with regard to his pay: he replied: "Do you think I came to India for the pay I receive?—I came to fulfil my duties as a Priest, and this is one of them." In this instance no official notice was taken; but here again the want of due regulations might have left the Chaplain at the mercy of a commanding officer, and have subjected him to the loss of the paltry sum allotted to him for his services, because he adhered to one of the regulations of his Church.

MODERN HISTORY OF THE MISSION OF MADURA.

It has been already said, that after the French revolution had prevented the Seminary for Foreign Missions, who succeeded the Jesuits, from sending out Priests, the Mission was supplied, from Goa, with Clergy far inferior, both in learning and virtue, to their predecessors; nor were they sufficiently numerous to have maintained religion on its former footing. The consequence was, that many Catholic communities, wearied with the neglect, the extortion, or the scandalous conduct of that brief generation of Clergy, joined the Protestants. The greater part of these have been happily won back already, and small as is the number of Priests in the district, this source of perversion is closed. But the evil had grown very great before 1837, when, in consequence of the petition presented to the Pope, of which mention has already been made, four Jesuit Missioners reached Madura. They had many and formidable difficulties to encounter, above all the schism, whose history is given in a previous chapter. The Goa Clergy made every imaginable effort to force the people to adhere to them, but often ineffectually, till the Missioner found himself obliged to check some abuse to which the people were attached, on which a whole village would join the schismatics. They also carried on numberless law suits for the churches, chapels and schools, to all which the Missioners laid claim, as the only lawfully constituted Catholic Clergy in the country. At one time they succeeded in getting a decree from the English Magistrate, declaring that all the churches and chapels in the district were their's by right. This was of course a great triumph, and the Catholics were at once expelled from above sixty churches; but the Magistrate had exceeded his powers, and the Catholics were enabled to continue this legal warfare, sometimes with success, but at very great expense. In many cases they have been forced to build new churches, usually very small, with mud walls and palm-leaf roofs, but sometimes really good buildings, superior to the old. Still the Indian attachment to what is ancient made the people cling to their former places of worship. The Protestant ministers, in most instances, aided the schismatical party, which often went to almost incredible lengths, in their opposition to the lawfully appointed Missioners. The Schismatics did not even scruple to use poison on more than one occasion, and two at least of the Missioners are believed to have died thus, whilst several others endured serious and repeated illness, attributed to the same cause. Nevertheless the schism was rapidly dying away, partly by the conversion of the greater portion of its supporters, partly from the gradual extinction of the Goa clergy, when, as has been related above, the new Archbishop of Goa arrived in India, and breaking all his oaths to the Holy See, revived and gave new vigour to this great evil. Still the schism is disappearing, and it is hoped that, in a few years more, it will be reckoned with the past.

In most places the house occupied by the Missioner when he comes is a mud hut, perhaps seven or eight feet wide by twelve in length, and about seven feet high, thatched with palm-leaves, without windows, without even a door, and without furniture of any kind, not so much as a table or a chair. If there is a board of any sort to be found, he spreads on it the mat, which is his only bed: his food is nothing but rice, and curry made of lean, tough fowls when they can be procured.

The immense size of the district adds much to the toils of the Priests, who are obliged by these law-suits, by sick-calls, and by the necessity of visiting in turn each of the widely scattered Christian villages, to be continually on the road. As far as possible they endeavour to remain several days together in each village, to instruct, to hear Confessions, to remedy abuses, &c. But then they must proceed to another, and thus they seldom have a fixed dwelling, and except at a few central stations they cannot afford time or money to attend to their own comforts, or to what we should consider the barest necessaries of life.

Amidst all these privations the Missioner must go through his duties; he must hear the confessions of all who come, and their numbers may be guessed at by the fact that, in the first year, above 8,000 were heard, aud now the Catholics are much more numerous; he must besides instruct the people as well as he can, and administer the other Sacraments. An instance of the kind of people they have to deal with may be worth relating. A Priest went to a village for the first time, and enquired of the assembled congregation if there were any children to be baptized: no one replied. After some minutes, one of the principal persons brought an infant, and when the ceremonies of the Christening were over, offered a small piece of money. The Missioner refused it, saying, he never took any payment for a Baptism: immediately children of all ages were brought in, and above fifty were Christened in one village.

With all this, time must be found to preach to the Heathens, and considering the other labours of the Clergy, their success in this is great. They do not neglect the mode of saving souls so largely adopted in all our Missions, that of baptizing dying children: in India the fondness of the parents prevents children being exposed as they are in China, and the Priest finds them principally by visiting the sick, and giving medicines as far as he can. Thus, as a physician of the body he often first gains access to a Pagan house or village, where, as a Christian preacher, he would have had no hearers.

Such is the life of men accustomed to European comforts, and often belonging to affluent families. Is it wonderful that such toils and hardships, in so trying a climate, should cost many lives? In the first ten years after the establishment of the Mission, twenty-one priests have died out of sixty-four, all of them young men, and most had not reached the age of 35. How many of these valuable lives might have been saved, if the funds of the Mission could have allowed them less wretched dwellings and better food? The deaths of some were so edifying that this sketch would be incomplete without a few details.

The first who died was Father Fidelis Alexander Martin, one of the four first sent out, and who had laboured with great zeal and success in the Mission. He had lately been made Superior of the Marava district, and was most beloved by the Christians, and feared by the schismatical party, on account of the numbers whom he won over to the truth. Frequently he reached a village at night, invited the people to Confession, sat in the Church hearing them till it was time to say mass next morning, then after eating a little food remounted his horse and continued his journey, taking no rest till the heat of the day obliged him to seek shelter. No remonstrance could make him take more care of his health; he often made good resolutions on the subject, but when anything was to be done they were all forgotten. In May 1840, the four Missioners met at Pallitama, and spent six days together making arrangements about their duties, &c. They separated on the 24th, and Father Martin went to celebrate the Feast of the Ascension in his own district. On the 30th, F. Bertrand received a summons to come and attend him, for he was dying: he was nearly fifty miles off, but he reached the neighbourhood by seven o'clock next morning, and heard from some people whom he passed, that F. Martin was better; so he entered a Church, and prepared to say Mass. The people began the prayers which are usually said before Mass, and as they finished, added — "and also for the soul of Father Fidelis Alexander." F. Bertrand instantly enquired, and found that he had died the previous evening. He could not wait even to say his Mass, but remounted his horse, and at nine o'clock reached the place where lay the body of his beloved friend. The calm face shewed that he had not died of cholera, which was then very prevalent, and to which he had exposed himself in every way in his constant attendance on the sick. The Christians were still weeping round the body, and Father Bertrand learned from them, that on the 28th—Ascension Thursday—he had felt ill, but insisted on proceeding to the next Christian village, and forbidding the people, who were alarmed at his symptoms, to send for one of the other Missioners, he insisted on saying Mass, and then hearing Confessions till he became so ill with dysentery that he was forced to lie down, and allowed them to send for F. Bertrand. On Saturday he was better for a few hours, but a fresh attack in the afternoon carried him off. He was perfectly resigned, and comforted his weeping flock, saying: "I did not come to this country to live in it for ever." He much regretted dying without the last Sacraments, but in this, as in all else, resigned himself completely to the will of God, and cast himself with trusting love into His divine Arms. He was buried in the enclosure which surrounds the Church. The attachment of his flock, his great reputation for sanctity, and the high respect in which he was held, have made the tomb an object of pilgrimage, and it is visited by thousands every year. The people loudly proclaim that very many sick have there been cured, but the circumstances have not been examined with sufficient care to allow of more than a statement of the popular belief. It seems, however, impossible to doubt that many who have undertaken this pilgrimage from great distances, so ill that their friends assured them they could never reach the end of their journey, have returned in health. There have been as many as fifteen thousand collected on the anniversary of his death, and though the Missioners are careful to restrain the veneration for him as far as may be, since he has not been beatified by the Holy See, yet it is an excellent opportunity of bringing numbers to the Sacraments, and reviving religious feelings in their hearts.

Father de Bournet, who had been but a few months in the country, and had been placed under Father Martin, survived him scarcely twenty days. He had received news of his friend's illness, and arrived too late; he and Father Bertrand spent five days together, and as they parted expressed a hope that this leave-taking might not be like that with F. Martin, never to meet again on earth, but added, "God's will be done." F. Bournet had proceeded through his district, and F. Bertrand set out to rejoin him some days later. On the 13th of June he received a letter from him, written in good health; that evening he learned that he was dying! He hurried forward, and found him alive, but very ill of a kind of nervous fever. Father Canoz, now Bishop of Madura, was with him, and for several days they watched beside the mat on which he lay, hoping sometimes that the worst was over, and edified by his perfect resignation, which was so entire that he refused to pray for recovery, but only that God's will might be done. He begged for Extreme Unction while they still had great hopes that he might be spared, saying it would give him courage to suffer as much as God pleased to send him. He continually repeated the prayer, "Jesus, Mary, Joseph, &c." and all the prayers suitable for a dying man, and on the night of Friday after Corpus Christi, 1840, he peacefully expired. The house resounded with the sobs of the Christians, who had already become much attached to him, and who felt that they had now lost a second most valuable guide in their path to Eternity.

Till February 1843 the Mission lost no more of its Priests, and several new ones had arrived from Europe. Among them was Father Alexander de St. Sardos, who reached Trichinopoly in June, 1841, and rapidly acquired the Tamul language, so that the Christians were delighted with his instructions; but he over-exerted himself deplorably in his zealous efforts to gain souls to God. He often spent whole days in the Confessional, deferring his Mass till a late hour, and then resuming his labours. He thought no length of time too great to gain a sinner who would not readily give up an enmity, or do whatever else might be necessary to make his Confession good. When the cholera broke out, he devoted himself to the sick, assisting them in every possible way, and when implored to take care of his own life, replied that he did not fear death; he endeavoured always to keep his soul ready to appear before God. On the 2nd of February, before he said his Mass, he attended a child of ten years old ill of the cholera, and after Mass had but little to eat, for he never cared what was set before him. He felt rather ill, but continued his usual duties till evening, when he was forced to give up: later, he sent a messenger to F. Combe, who was about twenty-five miles off; he then endeavoured to say his breviary, declaring that he must pray while he had strength; he told his Catechist that for several days he had felt a warning, while he was saying Mass, that he should not live beyond a few days. He then knelt before the altar, and offered his life to God. They brought some straw to spread his mat upon, and he lay down, to rise no more. His sufferings were very great, but he never complained; he expressed some anxiety that F. Combe might arrive in time, but it was in vain: he had been dead above an hour, though F. Combe had lost not a moment in setting out when he received the message.

On the 18th of the same month F. Chavignon was seized just as he was about to say Mass. He had been hearing Confessions till late the night before, and had had nothing to eat but a little rice. In the morning he continued his instructions to his flock, and then prepared to say Mass, though his Catechist warned him that he perceived symptoms of Cholera. Before he could begin he sunk against the altar. He was carried to his mat, and a messenger sent for F. Garnier, the nearest priest, who arrived at noon, and brought some remedies with him; but it was too late to save life, though he lingered till the morning of the 21st, perfectly resigned to the will of God, and never uttering a single word of complaint, though his sufferings were intense.

On the 5th July of this same year, 1843, died F. Louis Garnier, Superior of the Mission, and one of the four who came out in 1837. Nor was this the last loss the Mission sustained in that fatal year. On the 30th July died F. Peter Faurie, who had only arrived in India the preceding October. But the account of his last moments will be found in the letters of Father Clifford, in the next chapter. On the 16th of October died another of the young Missioners, Father Claude Deschamps, who had not been above two months in the country. He was very clever, and had made considerable progress both in English and in Tamul, but he suffered severely from headache, which at first he concealed, thinking it of no consequence. As soon as he mentioned it, physicians were consulted, but he continued to get worse till the 14th October, when he felt so weak that he begged to have the last Sacraments, though those around did not think him in immediate danger. He often exclaimed: "Oh! how pure we must be to appear before God! It is only at death that we can understand it." He then begged the prayers of the Missioners, and for some time was quite calm, but delirium came on, and lasted for thirty-six hours; it ceased before he expired, but he was speechless, and in the night of the 16th he died, to the deep regret of his companions, who had become truly attached to him, and had hoped much from his zeal and talent. He had long foreseen his death: indeed he left France with a conviction that his career would be short, and amid the sufferings and privations inseparable from a Missionary life he often exclaimed, "How happy I am! God is pleased to be satisfied with my good will, and to accept my sacrifice at once!"

Two more were yet to be added to the fatal list of that year. Father Louis du Ranquet was seized with cholera on the 7th of October; another of the Fathers, who was already on his way to meet him and confer about the state of the Mission, hurried forward on receiving the sad news, and arrived in time to hear his Confession and give him the last Sacraments; he received every attention that circumstances would allow, but on the 8th he peacefully expired.

Father Francis Perrin survived him but a few days. Like F. Deschamps, to whom he was much attached, he had been in the country but just twelve months, and was very young. The account of his death will be found in the letters of Father Walter Clifford.

For some months there was a respite, and the next who died, Father Clifford, requires a separate chapter.

In October 1845, died Father Louis Berlendis, an Italian of great zeal and talent, who had been the companion of the celebrated Cardinal Odescalchi after he had resigned his dignity to become an humble Jesuit. He foretold to F. Berlendis, that he would die in India, but this prophecy in no degree lessened his earnest desire to be sent on Foreign Missions. His health was very delicate, and in his journey across the isthmus of Suez, in February 1844, he had spat blood; the climate of India did not suit him as had been hoped; the privations made necessary by the poverty of the Mission pressed very severely on him, and in August he was so ill as to leave little hope. His admirable patience, and his loving conformity to the will of God, were most exemplary, and to the last his Superiors hoped he might be spared, as they knew how useful to the Mission his varied knowledge, and his acquaintance with the medical art would be. On the 4th of October, he received the last Sacraments, and died the following day, so happily that the survivors hardly dared regret one who so evidently exchanged his tedious sufferings for a better life.

Again some months passed without death's claiming fresh victims among the small number of Missioners who were labouring in this great harvest. But in July 1846 cholera again appeared, and carried off no less than four of the Fathers. The first was Father de St. Ferriol, who was attached to Pratacoudi, whither he had just returned after a journey to Negapatam to make a retreat. He sank within little more than twelve hours, dying July 19th.

On the same day at Negapatam, F. O'Kenny was seized with cholera. He was an Irishman, the only British subject on the Mission after the death of the Hon. and Rev. Walter Clifford, and had been sent out especially to assist in the College lately established in that town, as will be seen in a subsequent chapter. A few hours after his illness was known to be cholera, one of the boys in the school was also attacked, and in spite of every effort died on the following day. Father O'Kenny lingered some hours longer, and at one time there was a hope that he might recover, but it was in vain: he died July 21st.

Father Audibert had been ill even before F. O'Kenny, but his disease was not considered at first to be cholera. As soon as this was known, the boys in the school, who were excessively alarmed, were sent home, or entrusted to the friends of their parents. In spite of all that could be done F. Audibert, weakened by privations and by previous illness, was soon in a hopeless state. Till within a few hours of his death he was perfectly sensible, but then delirium came on, and after a violent attack he fell into his agony, which lasted an hour, when he peacefully expired, July 22nd.

The last victim was F. Barret, who had only landed with two companions at Pondicherry on the day of F. Audibert's death. They proceeded at once to Negapatam, F. Barret saying, when he heard of the sad state of things there: "My health is good enough for ordinary circumstances, but I can hardly hope to escape the cholera: perhaps I may be attacked as soon as I arrive: no matter; I have made my sacrifice." He was not mistaken: he was taken ill the very night he reached Negapatam, and next morning made his Confession, and begged to be allowed to make his vows, for he had but just completed his two year's novitiate, and having received the last Sacraments, he expired in sentiments of joyful hope.

Till 1849 the Mission was spared further losses by death; but in that year dysentery carried off Father Ponsdevier, a young Frenchman, who had been a lawyer of great promise before he joined the Society of Jesus. He made his novitiate in France, and then offered himself for the Foreign Missions, and proceeded to Negapatam, and thence to Trichinopoly, where he died of dysentery after about two years of labour in the Mission.

In 1850, cholera again claimed a victim, and this time also it was a young Priest, not ordained a year. Father Sartoris was a Savoyard by birth, and had proceeded to India before his noviceship was ended. He was one of the first Priests ordained by the present Bishop,

Dr. Canoz, and was much beloved by his companions. He had but just begun to labour among the Natives, when he was sent to a village where a violent dispute was raging, to endeavour to reconcile the adversaries. He was making some progress in this good work when he was seized with cholera, which was ravaging the village, and after a short illness died.

In 1851 another Priest was carried off by dysentery. Father Conneil was about 36 years of age, and had been in India about four years. In each of the years just mentioned, a young novice had also fallen a victim to cholera; they were young men from Goa, descended from Portuguese ancestors, and of great promise. One of them was of a very distinguished family in Goa, and their loss was almost as much felt by the Mission as that of the Priests whose deaths have been mentioned at greater length.

THE HON. AND REV. WALTER CLIFFORD.

This Father was brother to the present Lord Clifford, and was educated at the College of Stonyhurst. Feeling himself called to a religious life, he decided on joining the Society of Jesus, and his novitiate was made at Rome. Having completed it, he returned to England, was ordained Priest, and for some years laboured most zealously on the English Mission, and distinguished himself by his indefatigable exertions.

Being obliged to spend some time in France, he met some of the Fathers who had been on the Indian Mission, and conversed much with them. Up to that time he had been opposed to foreign Missions in general, saying that while there was so much to be done at home, and so few labourers, it was wrong to waste precious lives among heathen and savage nations. What he now saw and heard so completely changed his opinion, that, after making a retreat to ascertain what might be God's will in the matter, he felt himself called to offer for the foreign Missions, and was at once accepted and ordered to proceed to India. He did not even return to England to take leave of his friends and relations, but on the 23rd February, 1841, embarked with FF. Wilmot, de St. Sardos, and St. Cyr, on board the French ship "Ganges," at Bordeaux. For the first few days they suffered much from sea-sickness, but as soon as possible they laid down an arrangement of the day by which they might, in some degree conform themselves to their collegiate regulations, and on Sunday, March 7th, with the Captain's consent, they prepared a little altar in the cabin occupied by FF. Wilmot and St. Cyr, and said Mass; such as the crew as chose, and could find room, being allowed to attend. The space was so confined that, on the succeeding Sundays, the Captain had the altar placed against the mizen mast in the poop cabin, and there each Sunday, while the voyage lasted, the Holy Sacrifice was offered, in presence of most of the crew and passengers. On Easter day they were not far from the Cape of Good Hope, and the festival was celebrated by the first Communion of three of the sailors, whom the Missioners had instructed and prepared, and by several others fulfilling their Easter duties. Little more than a week after, F. Wilmot was seized with violent colic, which lasted for some days, and which returned so frequently that he could hardly be called well till he arrived in India. There was no physician on board, and the various remedies suggested in turn by those around gave little relief. His patience was most edifying, offering all his sufferings for the success of the voyage and the conversion of the Hindoos.

On the eve of Whit-Sunday, F. St. Cyr was up by four o'clock, and two sailors slipped quietly into his cabin to make their first Communion, for which they had been preparing for some time. At the beginning of the voyage they had refused all instruction, and one of them had his head filled with impious books. Grace had however triumphed over both, and their firm and decided characters gave great hopes that they would persevere. Their conversion was soon known throughout the ship, and excited much surprise. On Whit-Sunday two more stray sheep entered the fold of Christ: they were two of the officers, who had gone to sea very young, and had never lost their faith, though they had neglected their religious duties, and had not yet made their first Communion, which they now did in a most edifying manner. Two of the sailors also, who had not fulfilled their duties at Easter, did so now, and several who had, communicated again. One only of the whole crew had refused, almost to the last, to listen to instruction, but he too yielded before they reached the shores of India. They landed at Pondicherry on Whit-Monday, May 31st, after one of the most rapid voyages on record.

The arrival of Father Clifford was a great benefit to the Mission, which was entirely in the hands of French Priests, whose ignorance of English was a deplorable disadvantage in their intercourse with official persons, and whose true position had been much misunderstood. The presence of a clergyman of Father Clifford's rank tended much to prove that those with whom he was joined were really actuated by religious duty, and not by any sinister motives, in their struggles with the schismatics for the possession of the churches and property attached to the Mission. His zeal was of course smiled at as enthusiasm by the Protestants, but sincere enthusiasm commands respect even in those who do not share it, and it was soon seen that F. Clifford never hesitated to risk health or life for the interests of religion. Those who knew the difficulties he had to encounter were astonished at the quantity of work he got through, for some months performing the whole of the duties at Trichinopoly, not only among the soldiers, but also the native congregation, though his knowledge of Tamul could not be great in the short time he had been in the country. Two of his letters, which give an account of the deaths of two Missioners mentioned in the preceding chapter, will give a better idea of his natural kindness of heart, and of the state of the Mission, than can be conveyed in any other way. The first is addressed to the Superior in France, and is dated from

"Trichinopoly, July 31st, 1843.

"P. C.

"Rev. Father,

"A few days ago I begged F. Perrin, who was detained here on account of the prevalence of cholera in the district, which made the labour too great for me alone, to inform you of our terrible loss, by sending you a copy of F. Tassis' letter describing the last moments of our venerated Superior. Oh! Rev. Father, I cannot tell you how deeply I have felt the blow which has been sent us, and the more on account of the two other misfortunes which we had undergone this year, 1843! This third loss has pierced me to the heart. I did so love good F. Garnier! We suited each other so well! I know I have given way too much to grief: but Rev. Father, what would you have? I was so much attached to him. May God forgive me; may He cease to afflict us, and turn aside from us His wrath!

"We had a solemn service here at Trichinopoly, for the repose of F. Garnier's soul, on the 10th July, and we were obliged to celebrate a second on the following day, because our soldiers wished to be present, and they had not been able to do so the first day. On both occasions the crowd was great, and their tears very touching. They entreat so earnestly to have his body here that F. Bertrand cannot refuse, and it must be brought hither as soon as possible. It is only fitting that this good Father should repose in the centre of the Mission, in the church he built, at the foot of the altar he had just finished ornamenting. There were more than 500 Communions on the occasion of his death; our good Christians have set an example, which perhaps is seldom imitated in Europe, of the right way of lamenting a Pastor and shewing attachment to him, that is, to offer for the repose of his soul the spotless Victim of our redemption. The funeral ceremony concluded, according to the custom of the country, by the Catechist reading aloud the names of all the Fathers who have died in this Mission, and by prayers being again said for them.

"Alas! Rev. Father, I little thought then that a fresh name must soon be added to this melancholy list! The wound made in our hearts by F. Garnier's death was still bleeding when a new and scarcely less painful loss re-opened it. Our Lord has been pleased to call to Himself our dear F. Peter Faurie, who died here, at Trichinopoly, on the 30th July, the eve of St. Ignatius, our holy Father.

"This good Father had reached the country last October, as you know from our previous letters. He was sent first to Madura, and remained there, wholly occupied in studying Tamul, till January. He then went with F. Gury to Vadongarapathy, about thirty miles from Trichinopoly, that he might enter on his labours under the guidance of this excellent Missioner. His health was a good deal tried by the climate, and the precautions which the charity of his Superiors obliged him to take; the remedies which the country physicians gave him, did not produce the desired effect. Still we were far from thinking the evil as serious as it really was. He was re-called to Trichinopoly that he might be better looked after, and was attended by the English surgeon of the 94th Regiment, Mr. Turnbull, an excellent man, for whom I feel sincere esteem and gratitude. F. Perrin, who was then at Trichinopoly, and Brother Joseph Chevela, who lives there, gave him every care that the charity of the Society could suggest: I may add, that I myself spared no trouble, but all was vain. F. Perrin was seized with a dysentery which resisted all our efforts.

"He had for some time felt a secret presentiment of his death, and spoke openly of it: we could not succeed in reviving his hopes. A second physician, whom our surgeon had latterly brought with him, did not think the disease very serious; but the patient was obliged to take to his bed, and we saw that his strength declined rapidly. I thought it right to give him the last Sacraments on Friday evening, July 28. He received them calmly and peacefully, and from that moment conversed unceasingly with God, with the Blessed Virgin, and his holy Patrons. He was a most innocent being: a child of Mary. God was pleased to take him out of this world before the flower of virtue had been sullied by the dust of earth. *Raptus est ne malitia mutaret intellectum ejus.* Nothing could be more edifying than his last moments. Could you believe that he asked pardon, in my presence, and in that of the brethren, for all the faults he could tax himself with either here or in Europe? He charged me to tell you that he often thought particularly of your Reverence, and he also begged me to greet his poor mother and his family, and to beg you would comfort them for his death. I think a picture of the Blessed Virgin, which he constantly pressed to his heart, and kissed affectionately, will be a precious remembrance of him for his family. I will send you by the first opportunity this picture, his Crucifix and his rosary: also his theological notes, which he himself meant for his brother Francis. I repeated the absolutions several times, for he often thought the last moment was come. He would say: 'I am going; I am stifling:

pray for me.' A moment before he breathed his last I gave him absolution once more, and while I was saying the prayer, '*Anima Christi*,' and repeating two or three times the words, 'command me to come to Thee,' he peacefully gave up his soul to Jesus, whose sacred Heart he had unceasingly invoked, as well as that of our loving Mother Mary.

"In the evening our brave soldiers carried the body on their shoulders from the house to the Church, amid a crowd of Christians, who, grieved to their inmost souls at seeing us thus fall one after another, sacrificing ourselves for them, filled the air with their cries and lamentations. It was left all night laid out in the midst of the Christians, who watched and prayed round the bier. In the morning I said Mass, and performed the obsequies according to our customs. Our soldiers and a crowd of Christians, were present, showing their grief for this fresh loss by their tears and fervent prayers. It was a touching sight, Rev. Father; my very heart was moved by this unanimous cry of a whole people, sent up to the Father of mercy, beseeching Him to have pity on one who had wished to be the Minister of His goodness towards them, if His adorable designs had allowed. This prayer of a people simple in their faith, and perhaps deserving by this very simplicity our Lord's praise, *I have not found such faith in Israel*, will surely have been heard and granted in Heaven! May their cries one day resound in this holy temple, and thence mount to the throne of grace for my soul! I ask nothing better than to die in India, like the good Father whose loss we deplore, *in osculo Domini: Amen! Amen!* He rests beside F. Charignon, near the altar on the epistle side; and I am confident that, with them, FF. Garnier and St. Sardos have this day kept, in the house of our Heavenly Father, a far more brilliant and joyous festival of our holy Patriarch St. Ignatius, than we have had here in this land of exile.

But whatever anguish we may feel, do not fear, Rev. Father, that the death of our beloved brothers and comrades will make us lose courage, or look backwards. Could we view thus wrongly an end so precious before the Lord? God preserve us from so far forgetting our honour as to feel the least hesitation. Let us be ready to die fighting for God. Let us not turn our glory into shame by shrinking from the Cross, in which is our safety; our life, and our resurrection. I perhaps felt too natural and sensible a grief for the death of F. Garnier: that of F. Faurie, which I have just witnessed, far from having the same effect on me, fills me with the sweetest consolation. I shall never forget the filial piety with which he kissed the picture of the Blessed Virgin, his good Mother, and the reliquary of our Father St. Ignatius, nor the expression of faith, sweetness and resignation with which his dying eyes were fixed on me, while I was recommending his soul to the sacred Heart of Jesus, which he so tenderly loved and invoked. May this death then encourage us all to go forward in the path which leads to our eternal country. *Festinemus ingredi in illam requiem.*

"As a last circumstance I must add that our dear F. Faurie preserved his senses to his last breath, and at that moment he was as calm and collected as if he had been about to receive the Holy Communion. How sweet it is at that last instant to have been, during life, the faithful servant of the Mother of God! How comforting to die a child of the Society, in whatever place we may be, in Europe, Asia, Africa, or America, wheresoever obedience and the will of God may have placed us.

"Rev. Father, pray for me that I may obtain final perseverance, from the sacred Heart of Jesus, through the intercession of Mary, and of my holy Patrons SS. Peter, Ignatius, Xavier and Stanislaus; that I may, sinner as I am, die like this good Father whom we lament, repeating from my heart: 'Command me to come to Thee, that with Thy saints I may praise Thee, for ever and ever. Amen.' I recommend myself, therefore, to the Masses and prayers of your Reverence, and of all our Fathers and Brothers, and I beg you to accept the assurance of my profound respect, &c.

(Signed) "WALTER CLIFFORD, S. J."

The next letter is dated also from Trichinopoly, November 18, 1843, and is addressed to the Father Provincial.

"P. C.

"Rev. Father,

"The Indian mails have several times brought you sad news, informing you of the sickness or death of some of our Missioners. This one will renew your grief, by announcing the double loss we have just sustained, of two of our dear fellow-labourers. It has pleased the Lord to deprive us of FF. Louis du Ranquet and Francis Perrin, both carried off by cholera, the former at Strivegondom, near Palamcotty, on the 8th of November; the latter at Trichinopoly, on the 12th of this same month. I will say nothing of F. du Ranquet, because F. Wilmet, in whose arms he breathed his last, has undertaken this account: but I will tell you about F. Francis Perrin, to whom I gave the last consolations of religion. From the time of his arrival in India he was busy studying Tamul, and as we mentioned in our last letters was in good health. He had interrupted this employment for some days to make his annual retreat, and prepare for the Feast of St. Stanislas Kostka, which we were to celebrate on the 13th of November. On Saturday the 11th he felt unwell, but thought it of no consequence, and said nothing. The following night he was seized with a sudden coldness, a symptom of cholera. As soon as ever I heard of his illness, I sent for an English Physician, who attended him with the greatest care, but all was useless; the attack was too violent, and the disease became worse. The Father Superior himself was ill in bed, and I, therefore, gave F. Perrin the last Sacraments. I need not tell you, who knew his piety, that he rereceived them with the most perfect dispositions. During his retreat he had a feeling that God required him to make a complete sacrifice of himself, and he did so with his whole heart, and with all his will. 'What a happy day for me!' he exclaimed, while we were praying, bathed in tears, round his bed of suffering; 'What a happy day for me! Do not weep, I am going to Heaven!' I shall never forget what I felt when I saw him lift his hands and eyes to Heaven with the most moving affection and the most perfect resignation to the will of God, when I suggested to him to unite his intentions in his last moments with those of our Saints, and to enter into the sentiments they had at the hour of death: 'in particular,' I added, 'those of F. Claude Deschamps, your companion in your journey, who has already gone before you to glory.' How this thought touched him, and filled him with a sweet confidence that he would soon see his friend again in a better world! In these dispositions he calmly gave up his soul to God on the 12th November, about half-past eight o'clock in the evening.

"I think we might inscribe on the tomb of these two dear and fervent fellow-novices the beautiful words of the Church: *As in life they loved one another, so in death they are not* divided. Their souls will be re-united in Heaven, as their bodies have been on earth. Let us hope that it may be so. Meanwhile, faithful to what fraternal charity requires of us, let us pray that this inestimable grace may soon be granted to them, and that they may enter without delay that happy dwelling in which suffering and death are feared no more.

"I must now recommend the whole Mission, and each of its members, to the Masses and prayers of the whole Province. It is easy to understand how much we need this help, when we have death so continually before our eyes, amid the ravages of cholera, among persons who are in good health to-day, and whom we see lying on their biers a few hours after.

"I have the honour to be, &c.,

(Signed) "WALTER CLIFFORD, S.J."

These numerous deaths gave great weight to the remonstrance which, from the moment he became acquainted with the Mission, F. Clifford had made against the excessively severe lives led by the Priests. Such privations were no longer necessary to win for them the respect and confidence of the natives, which had been the principal motive of F. Robert de Nobili, and others of the early Missioners, in laying down such rigid rules. The number of Europeans of all classes settled there, and the power acquired by European nations, has now completely accustomed the people to modes of life entirely different from their own; in many respects the strong line of demarcation between the castes is lessened, and a Pariah need no longer crawl in the dust before a Brahmin. Provided a European Priest avoids shocking their peculiar prejudices by eating beef, &c., they do not respect him less for continuing, in some degree, the diet they know he was accustomed to. But till F. Clifford's arrival, the Jesuits in Madura never tasted meat, or wine, but lived entirely on rice and fish, and often so little of these that some now living can remember repeatedly fainting from exhaustion as they said Mass in the morning. Even bread was a luxury almost unknown, for in every respect they lived as the poorer class of natives. This, joined to the excessive toil they often underwent, spending hours in the Confessional, and in giving instructions, riding long journeys from one Christian village to another, and having no better resting place on their arrival than the wretched hut which has been described, was too much for the strength of men accustomed to better food, and in sufficient quantity, and made them an easy prey to cholera, or any other disease by which they might be attacked. Again and again F. Clifford remonstrated with the Superiors in France; the poverty of the Mission was such as to make it difficult to improve the diet without taking from other purposes no less necessary. Large sums were required in defending the Catholic interests in the lawsuits constantly carried on against them by the ecclesiastics for the possession of the churches and chapels built by their European predecessors in the Mission; and the Priests themselves were most unwilling to spend on their own maintenance anything beyond what was absolutely necessary. At length, however,

F. Clifford succeeded in obtaining an order to allow themselves a small quantity of wine daily, and meat every day except Fridays, Saturdays, and the fast-days of the Church, and bread in moderate quantity, but sufficient to prevent actual suffering from hunger—a great change from the days when five farthings' worth of fish, with rice and a few mouthfuls of bread, was considered enough for the dinner of six Priests. F. Clifford represented, among other arguments, the great expense of sending out fresh Missioners to replace those who died, and that it would cost far less to allow them a proper maintenance. The consequence has been what he expected: as soon as this improved diet began to tell on the constitutions of the Priests, the deaths became far less numerous, and for the last few years the mortality has not more than doubled that in easier Missions.

F. Clifford never spared himself when he could hope to win souls to God. Being the first English Priest who had been in the district, he soon acquired much influence with the Catholic soldiers of the European Regiments stationed at Trichinopoly, and revived religious feelings in their hearts. For some time he had charge both of them and of the native congregation, with whom he succeeded wonderfully, considering that he never became very familiar with the Tamul language. But he was not long spared. In the fatal year 1843 he had a slight threatening of cholera, caught in attending the sick, but it passed off, and his health continued pretty good till May 1844, when to the grief of the whole Mission he was drowned in bathing. The account of his death sent by F. Canoz, now Vicar Apostolic in Madura, to the Provincial in France, is worth inserting here. F. Canoz was on his way from Marava to Trichinopoly when he heard of the accident. He says—

"I learned on my road the sad news of the death of Father Clifford. This zealous Father cherished a hope of dying of cholera caught in attending the sick, which death was in his eyes the most desirable next to martyrdom. He never spared himself, and we often admired his generosity in flying to cholera patients. But God, whose judgments are impenetrable, had otherwise disposed: death awaited him in the water, which it is said he feared. On the 21st of May he set out from Trichinopoly to visit F. Bedin, and rested during the noon-day heat in a grove near the river Coliron, in which he thought he should like to bathe. He sent away his Hindoo attendants, and went into the water. As he did not know how to swim, he should have had the depth of the spot tried; but this precaution probably seemed needless to him. The poor Father stayed so long in the water that his attendants got uneasy, and went to the place where they had left him. They found nothing but his clothes on the river-bank; surprised and grieved, they searched the water long, but to no purpose. At length, when night came on, they hastened to tell F. Bedin, who was not above three miles off. He came instantly, bringing with him fishermen, who sought all night long, but with no better success. It was not till sun-rise that one of them, who had cast his net in the deepest spot, found the body. They took it at once to Trichinopoly, where it was buried; all the soldiers whose Chaplain F. Clifford had been, were present, as were all the authorities of the place, thunderstruck at this tragical death: the soldiers begged leave to erect him a funeral monument at their own expense. F. Clifford had always been very zealous for the salvation of the soldiers, and this year had succeeded in bringing to Confession several who had long neglected the Sacraments. On Sundays he usually preached with an earnestness which moved the most hardened. . . . . .

"What more shall I tell you, Rev. Father, of this fresh blow that has been sent us? As for its victim, we may lessen your grief by assuring you that we have no uneasiness. F. Clifford had a most tender conscience, and he had been to Confession at Trichinopoly the very day before this lamentable accident. Moreover the Lord, who in His mercy was perhaps pleased to spare him the trial of a lingering death, which he much feared, seems to have given him a kind of presentiment of his approaching end. Three days before this misfortune a Christian had come to see him, and, contrary to his habit of never allowing long conversations, he spoke with him for nearly an hour and a half on spiritual subjects, and especially on the necessity of being always ready to die. Thus prepared by Providence, and animated with a most lively faith, there can be no doubt that he made at that moment generous acts, which might supply for the usual helps of religion. It is true that viewing it with the eyes of Faith we should have preferred seeing him die of cholera caught among the sick, according to his own wish, but Providence has arranged otherwise for the common good of all. If we may use the expression, he deserved such a death for the generosity with which he braved it, but it might perhaps have alarmed us more, as being a fresh proof of what the rest had to fear.

"It cannot be concealed that this death is in itself a great loss to the Mission. The name of F. Clifford was respected by the English: it was a support for us in case of need with the government and the magistrates on whom we depend. We counted on him for the college we intend to establish: he would have drawn pupils to it, and directed the studies. God's holy will be done. If you can replace him by another English Father, you will do us a great service: an Englishman will always succeed better than we can with his own nation, whose manners, customs, and character he knows thoroughly."

F. Clifford himself had written to one of his sisters only three days before his death, consoling her for the loss of one of her sons, and he used these words, rendered remarkable by the event. "In the midst of life we are in death: who knows? perhaps the next post may bring you news that I too am no more." And it was so.

THE COLLEGE OF NEGAPATAM.

Father Clifford's anxiety for the foundation of a College, and the degree in which he was himself likely to have been useful to its working, have been alluded to in the foregoing letter. His death, and the other losses the Mission sustained, deferred its commencement till 1845, when a Seminary College, chiefly in the hope of training the future Clergy of the district, was opened at Negapatam. This city stands on a branch of the river Cavery, in the kingdom of Tanjore, in the Southern part of India. There had been a Seminary there formerly, which was one reason for its selection as a site. Poor as the Mission was, and with very few Priests, it was absolutely necessary to open this School without delay, as the children of Catholic parents, having no means of education, were daily enticed into exceptionable schools, where not only their Faith but, in some instances their morals also were the sacrifice. The immense sums expended by the various Protestant sects have been alluded to in a previous chapter. We find the following estimate in a well-known Journal:

"REVENUES OF MISSIONARY SOCIETIES.—The London Missionary Society commenced its operations in 1800, and up to 1849 it had expended £ 1,922,346 : 18 : 2. The Baptist Missionary Society commenced also in 1800, and up to 1842 it had expended £ 620,431 : 11 : 9. The Wesleyan Missionary Society commenced in 1803, and had expended up to 1819 £ 2,269,855 : 9 : 0. The Church Missionary Society commenced in 1805, and had expended up to 1849 £ 2,153,750 : 18 : 11. The Society for Promoting Christianity among the Jews commenced in 1809, and up to 1849 it had expended £ 524,720 : 11 : 4. The British Society for Promoting Christianity among the Jews commenced in 1845, and up to 1849 had expended £ 12,028 : 10 : 0. The British Missions commenced in 1819, and up to 1849 had expended £ 169,965 : 15 : 9. The Moravian Missions obtain an average income from England of £ 3,000 a-year, which, for fifty years, is £150,000. The City of London Missions (home missions) commenced in 1836, and to 1849 it had expended £114,811 : 14 : 10; total, £8,007,921 : 11 : 6. To which must be added the income from all sources of the Society for the Propagation of the Gospel in Foreign Parts during the same period, £3,000,000. Grand total, £11,007,921 : 11 : 6.—*Herald.*"

Now with these incredible appliances and munitions for the spiritual war, it appears that they themselves estimated in 1849 the total number of their converts at only 32,000 souls, acknowledging that a great proportion of these are still half-pagans. Catholics would consider most of them wholly such, as they are not baptized, or likely to be so, and often have no other claim to Christianity than the insertion of their names in the Missionary's list, and sometimes the receipt of a pension for having it so placed. It is grievous to see so much money wasted with scarcely any, even nominal, benefit, while Catholic Schools cannot be founded for want of funds! In the Madura district alone there are forty European ministers of the various Protestant sects; four Native ones; above four hundred catechists; as many school-masters and school-mistresses; almost numberless day-schools; and ten seminaries, in which they collect as many pupils as they can, and give them education, books, lodging, clothes, and food gratuitously; yet with all this a Heathen is hardly ever permanently converted, and the children of Catholic parents frequently return to their true faith when they leave the schools.

Can Catholics remain idle while Protestants make such enormous efforts? There are at least 150,000 Catholics in the district of Madura, but almost all of them too poor to contribute anything like sufficient for the support of the Missioners, however inexpensively they may live. One-twentieth part of the sums spent annually by the Protestant Missions would suffice to maintain the Catholic one in affluence, to found schools and colleges, to educate young natives for the Priesthood, or to train them as Catechists, and thus would rapidly bring the Heathens into the fold of Christ. There would be no difficulty in getting pupils, no need of bribes to persuade them to attend: the Catholic parents will of course prefer Catholic schools when they are accessible, and the high caste Hindoos are more ready to send their sons to Catholic than to Protestant schools —first, because the mode of life of the Catholic Missioner is such as wins their respect far more than that of the Protestant, with his wife, his comfortable establishment, and Pariah servants; and secondly, because in the Catholic schools more care is taken to avoid outraging those customs of caste which have no necessary connection with Heathenism. Europeans will hardly believe how small a sum is sufficient for the support of a Native pupil: £4 a-year will usually be enough—and is it possible that Catholics will refuse this? Anyone giving as much as will produce £4 annually will thus have one scholar permanently in the College— one who may become a Native Priest, and contribute to the salvation of thousands; or if not called to so high a vocation, or not fitted for it by his talents, he may become a Catechist or a School-master—thus preparing the way for the Priest to follow and complete the good work of which he has sown the seeds; or thirdly, he may qualify himself for an employment under Government, and by his position and influence may contribute powerfully to defend the Catholics, still so often unjustly oppressed and misrepresented by the Heathens, the Schismatics, and the Protestant preachers; or at the very least he may become a good father of a family, and by his education acquire influence in his village, by his example contribute to make others live as Christians should, and thus consolidate religion in India.

The principal, or rather at present the only College in which this good work has been really begun is the one spoken of at the beginning of this chapter, opened at Negapatam in 1845. Only two Fathers could then be spared from the more active duties of the Mission, and though their pupils were not very numerous, the toil was beyond their strength. F. Audibert, whose death has been mentioned in a previous chapter, sunk under it, for he never regained his strength after the illness which seized him during the first year of his College labours, and died the year following of cholera.

The year 1846 opened with the happiest prospects to the College. More pupils were offered than could find room, but sixty-five were received, whose good conduct and diligence gave great hopes for their future career. This was interrupted by the breaking out of cholera, when three of the Fathers were carried off, and six of the scholars were attacked, two of whom, a Native boy and an Armenian, died. The latter was the hope of his family. The utmost terror now pervaded the school. The boys were immediately sent to their parents and relations; those who had none near were removed under the care of F. Tassis to Karical, and the alarm subsided; but the College was closed for three months. On its re-opening, few pupils appeared; but this was fully expected after such a fearful interruption.

On the 14th of September, 1849, the Feast of the Exaltation of the Cross, the first stone of the large building now used as the College was laid. Each of the Fathers, and each of the pupils, European and Native, came in succession, and placed a stone in the foundation; the funds for its erection were very small, but Providence blessed them, so that it gradually progressed, though the Mission was poorer than ever, because the political disturbances in France almost dried up the principal sources of its support. In the night of the 11th of September, 1849, the temporary dwelling in which the College was carried on was set on fire by the Schismatics, who had long been jealous of the strength it gained for the Catholic cause, and the attention it drew. All the inmates were asleep, but happily no lives were lost, though a few minutes were enough to wrap in flames the whole slight building, roofed only with cocoa-nut leaves. Of course the first object was to save the pupils, and so rapid was the progress of the conflagration that scarcely anything else was rescued. All the furniture, the library which was well-chosen and pretty numerous, in short, all they possessed, even to the greater part of their clothes, was destroyed. This crime was certainly committed by the Schismatics; there were proofs quite sufficient to have brought it home to them legally, but it was not followed up actively, and no punishment was inflicted.

F. de St. Cyr, the Superior, with characteristic energy, saw plainly that they must contrive to carry on the establishment with as little interruption as possible; he used for this purpose all the money he could in any way command, and trusted to Providence to enable him to pay such debts as were unavoidably incurred. There was a general feeling in its favour among the Protestants and Hindoos, as well as among the Catholics, and the works were pushed forward so energetically that thirteen days after the fire Mass was celebrated in the new chapel, and five days later all the Fathers, and their pupils, were established in the new temporary building. The great expense of buying afresh so many articles indispensable for daily use entailed severe privations on the Fathers, who endeavoured, by denying themselves in every possible way, to spare the very limited funds of the Mission, and contrive to go on with the College. They did not leave off the erection of the permanent one, and were helped by subscriptions from Europe, small in amount, but so unexpected as to give them great encouragement; subscriptions were also raised in the country, and about Easter 1850 a portion of the house was habitable. Early in 1851 the Fathers, and the pupils of European origin were established in it, while the Indian boys and their teachers remained in the temporary dwelling. The college is however quite unfinished, and would still require at least £1000 to complete it, without including the church. If these were erected in a suitable manner, religion would be benefitted even by the existence and outward appearance of buildings worthy of their destination.

The event proved that F. St. Cyr judged wisely in insisting on retaining the pupils, and urging on the erection of a temporary building, instead of breaking up the establishment, as some of the Fathers wished, till the new college could be used. The schismatics, seeing that the Missioners were not to be driven from their post, lost courage, and became far less violent, and many of them were converted; the Catholics gained confidence, and several of the English residents shewed by acts of kindness their appreciation of such resolute conduct: some of them, not quite liking, as Protestants, to give openly to Catholic Priests, offered loans of money, the payment of which they afterwards refused, and in short this great misfortune has been absolutely a benefit in its results to the cause it was intended to destroy. The pecuniary loss still weighs most heavily on the Mission, it is true, but in other respects the advantages were very considerable.

ACTUAL STATE OF THE MISSION.

In order to form a correct idea of the actual state of the Mission, it will be well to examine briefly what good has been done of late years. For greater clearness the district may be divided into three parts, Northern, Central, and Southern.

The Northern part contains three principal towns, Trichinopoly, Tanjore, and Negapatam.

Trichinopoly is within four miles of the river Cauvery, which is the Northern boundary of the Mission. It is a large military station, with a garrison of one company of European Artillery men in the Hon. Company's service; one regiment of European Infantry; two Sepoy regiments; and often a regiment of Native Cavalry. It contains about a hundred thousand inhabitants, Christians, Hindoos, and Mussulmans. The number of Christians is about eight thousand, consisting of Indo-Britons, or half-castes, Tamoulars, and Pariahs. The very great majority of the two first are Catholics, but there are many Pariahs who still follow the schismatic Priest. The Catholic church is large, well-built, and rather handsome. It was constructed by Rev. F. Garnier, one of the first Superiors of the modern Mission, at an expense of several thousand rupees, unaided by Government. The ceremonies of religion are performed in their church with all possible care, and as much splendour as can be afforded. Care and attention to this point has contributed very much to awaken feelings of piety in the native Christians, and to attract others to our holy religion: the impression produced by them is often very strong, as must naturally be the case with a people of such impressible character, and so fond of exterior show, as are the natives of India. On one occasion an old pensioned Sepoy, who had just been converted, came to assist for the first time at High Mass. He was so struck and delighted, that he declared it to be an image of Heaven, and began to use all his influence for the conversion of his friends. A retreat and mission given at Trichinopoly in 1845, and several private retreats*

* A retreat is a means of sanctification used in the Church in all ages, but brought into more frequent use, and fully systematized by St. Ignatius of Loyola, in his book called the "Spiritual Exercises." It consists of from three to eight days, or even a month, according to the wants and wishes of the individual, spent in private prayer and medi-

subsequently given to the catechists assembled from all parts of the Mission, and to the Christians of the city who wished to assist, have been productive of very great and almost unexpected advantages. The constant residence of one or more Priests at Trichinopoly, with the frequent presence of the Bishop, has likewise been productive of much good. The con-

tation, wherein the soul is spiritually exercised, and brought to a knowledge of the true end of her creation, and the means of attaining it. A mission is a retreat given to a large number of persons, often to a whole town, in which the private meditations are exchanged for public sermons on the great truths of religion. In the first part the soul is made sensible of what really is the end of her creation and existence in this life; the heinousness of sin is then explained by the *consequences* of the fall of man, that is, the *sufferings of this life*, and the *necessity* of the death of Jesus Christ to redeem and save him; *death, judgment, and hell* are meditated on. The necessity of struggling against the passions is then laid before the soul, and Christ, in His life on earth, is meditated upon deeply, as the model for the life of a Christian soldier. By reflecting on the Passion of our Divine Redeemer, the soul is encouraged to embrace generously the struggle for salvation, and to follow Christ as a leader, refusing no labour, no effort, to observe the holy law which He has died to establish. Heaven, and the joys of Christ's glorious Resurrection and Ascension, are then deeply meditated, in order to give courage and hope to the soul to go on cheerfully in the path of the Divine law, and thereby merit a participation of the glories reserved for those who are faithful unto death.

gregation is, on the whole, nearly as well organized, and gives as much consolation to their Pastors as most parishes in Europe. If we may judge by the immense increase, within the last few years, of annual and monthly communicants, and the daily attendance at Mass, there is indeed much to make the Missioner deeply thankful to heaven, and much to comfort him in his labours. Every Sunday and holiday there is an English sermon in the morning for the troops, and a Tamul sermon for the natives; and in the afternoon again, Catechism in Tamul for the natives, and either an English instruction, with Benediction, for the Europeans, or Vespers and Benediction.

As the Chaplaincy of the troops, and the good to be effected thereby, will form a chapter of itself, the native Mission only will here be spoken of.

Several of the French Missioners have shewn much tact in the judicious use of those exterior means of awakening piety in the soul so much in use on the continent. The ceremony of first Communions, which takes place every year, is prepared by the French Fathers with all that holy attention to devotional forms and ceremony which they so well understand, and which is even more useful, and productive of more good on the easily impressed minds of the Indians than it has produced at home. More than any other people perhaps the Indian appreciates a thing according as he sees it valued by others, and this will at once explain how useful well-ordered ceremony and show must be to form his mind to a due respect for holy things. The Christians in the immediate environs of Trichinopoly are far from offering the same consolation to the Missioner; they are too much dispersed to make it possible to assemble them frequently together, either for instruction or the Sacraments. There is however, at some distance to the West of Trichinopoly, a small district containing about six thousand Christians, which has made much progress in the last few years, during which a Priest has been permanently located amongst them. The people have begun to assist regularly at Mass on Sundays; to attend to and take an interest in religious instruction; and to frequent the Sacraments: their moral conduct has very much improved. The Priest having obtained a small fund of a few rupees for the purpose, assembled together all the children who were to make their first Communion, and fed and lodged them previously for three days, giving them at the same time ample instructions, and making them thoroughly learn their prayers, and the elements of religion: the usual examination followed this little retreat, and the intelligence, fervour and devotion of the children most fully repaid the Missioner for the trouble he had taken and the additional privations he had subjected himself to in order to meet the expense. It would be most desirable to organize this good work regularly in every part of the Mission; but the total want of funds has hitherto rendered it quite impossible to do so.

The district of Aöur, to the South of Trichinopoly, is far from presenting the same consoling spectacle. It contains about twelve thousand Christians in a district of about forty miles long by thirty broad; nearly one-third of these are schismatics. In this district is situated the famous church of Aöur, built by Father Bouchet, as described before. It is still unfortunately in the hands of the schismatics, and thus the Catholics, though far more numerous, are deprived entirely of a church supported for many years at their expense, and originally built by a European Jesuit Father, with his own funds.

To the East is the fertile district of Tanjore, the garden of Southern India. It contains about 25,000 Christians, in the midst of a very large and rich Heathen population. At some distance from the town are three small churches, built of brick: two were recovered from the Schismatics some time ago, and the third has just been constructed by subscription in a district of about 2,000 Christians, who have, for many years, been entirely neglected. In many parts of the country, when a new Church is raised, a congregation starts up around it, in a way that much astonishes the Missioner. The presence of some half-dozen Christian families induces the Missioner to erect a small temporary Church, which is no sooner established than several other families present themselves, and demand Baptism for their children, stating that their ancestors were Christians, and that they themselves were so in their infancy. The falling off of these families proceeds entirely from the interruption of the Mission for so many years. These people, though they have ceased to be Christians from want of religious instruction, have ever preserved a love and esteem for Christianity, and a very strong traditionary respect and affection for the European Priests who converted their ancestors to the faith. The moment an opportunity offers they return, as it were instinctively, to Christianity. Great indeed must have been the zeal and piety, the talents and efforts, of those who first planted Christianity amongst them, when nearly half a century after their complete disappearance, the very memory of their name is such an assistance to their successors.

The city of Tanjore is one of the great bulwarks of Hindooism in Southern India. The fort, with a small circuit round it, nominally does not belong to the East India Company, but remains in the possession of the hereditary Native Prince, who receives an immense pension from the Government. Nearly all his wealth is squandered on the Brahmins, and in Hindoo religious ceremonies on the most splendid scale. The old Catholic Church, at a short distance from the town, is still in the hands of the Schismatics. It was erected on a piece of ground given by the Rajah, many years ago, to a Jesuit Missioner in reward for some services. Within a couple of hundred yards is the temporary building at present used as a Catholic

Church: it is vast, but quite insufficient for the congregation, and entirely composed of clay and palm-leaves. The residence of a zealous Missioner, with active and well-disposed catechists, has produced during the last year an immense good for religion in this district. Repeated efforts had previously been made to reform these Christians, many of whom were of low caste, and nearly all in the service of Heathens, but in vain. At last a Confraternity was established similar to that of *Notre Dame des Victoires* at Paris, in which prayers were regularly offered up for the conversion of sinners: the effect was quite wonderful, the whole face of the district was changed, and instructions were regularly attended to on Sundays; the Sacraments were frequented; those at variance were reconciled; and scandals were suppressed. A great number of Schismatics, and several Heathens, were also converted to the holy Catholic faith.

Another most efficacious means for conversion amongst the Natives is the representation of the Passion of our Divine Redeemer, either by means of transparent pictures shewn at night with a light behind, or by a sort of commemorative exhibition, accompanied by a sermon. The intelligent reader will see how forcibly the Native is likely to be affected by such means. Everything is done with the greatest decorum and piety: and surely He who in mercy deigned to die in reality for our sins cannot object to have His death and sufferings pourtrayed in a manner *found to be efficacious,* in order to move the heart of the sinner to conversion and holiness of life. Many who have been proof against every exhortation and threat, have yielded, and cast themselves in tears of penitence at the feet of the Preacher, when witnessing one of these representations of the Passion of our Divine Redeemer. The genius and disposition of the Indian are entirely different from those of the European, and as far as human efforts are concerned in the spread of Christianity, the great secret is to take people according to their genius and disposition. The object of the Catholic Missioner in India is to make Christians of the Indians, that is, to make Indian Christians, who must, therefore, in all their manners, customs and feelings, save and except where the essential truths of religion are concerned, differ entirely from their European brethren. For instance, processions at night, accompanied by immense torches, noise, fireworks, and barbarous music, are neither Catholic nor Protestant, nor necessarily Heathenish, but they are *essentially Indian*, and therefore perfectly lawful for the Indian Catholic, as long as the object for which they are made is Christian and Catholic. The reader is therefore entreated not to judge the working of an Indian Mission by European ideas, but wisely and humbly to consider that those who, for no human motives, have devoted their talents and lives to the prosecution of the work of the conversion of the Indian, and who have the tradition of their *confrères'* experience during three hundred years to guide them, are better able to judge, on the spot and in the country, what is expedient and right, than those at home can possibly be.

The good effect of joining in an association of prayers under the protection of the Blessed Virgin was, as has been stated, most evident in Tanjore. A procession was made by the Christians to return thanks to God; and even the Heathens of the neighbourhood, edified and struck by a change so apparent in the conduct of their neighbours, freely contributed to the expenses of the festival, and joined in it as far as they were allowed. Unfortunately in this district there is a large body of nominal Catholics who gain their living as musicians, many of their wives and children are really well disposed, but the husbands are obliged, by custom all-powerful in India, to be present as musicians at all the festivals of the neighbourhood, whether Heathen or other. This concurrence can in no way be sanctioned by religion, being expressly forbidden by the Bull of Benedict XIV, ordering the excommunication of any such person. However, as they declare that they have no other means of subsistence, they persevere in resisting the advice of their Pastor, and no other punishment can be inflicted upon them than refusing them the Sacraments. Otherwise they would abandon even the semblance of religion, and force their wives and children to do the same; for the sake of these latter some forbearance has hitherto been shewn to these unfortunate men.

One of the greatest wants of this district at present is a large and respectable Church, such as may inspire by its appearance some esteem for the religion to which it belongs. How often, even in Europe, has a new impetus been given to religion in a district by the erection of a handsome church; the opportunity for this result, of awakening inward respect by outward means, exists in a far greater degree in India than in any other country.

The city of Tanjore is full of the most magnificent temples, and immense sums are daily expended there, in performing the ceremonies of Hindoo worship; whilst the holy Catholic faith is confined to a poor shed, little better than the stable of Bethlehem. This draws discredit and disrespect on our holy faith. In the whole of this portion of the Mission there is not a single decent church, nor a Missioner's residence to be compared in comfort to the cantonment hut of a married private soldier.

Another source of much discomfort to our Christians, and of trouble to the Missioner, is the forced contribution of money and labour for the support of Hindoo festivals, laid upon the Catholics by their Hindoo masters, and fellow-villagers.

A *vari* or tax is usually imposed on each house for this purpose, by a long established custom. The Christians are obliged, as a matter of course, not to pay this tax, which is in itself voluntary, and cannot be legally enforced; yet many would willingly pay it, in order to avoid the serious persecution to which a refusal on their parts would subject them from their fellow-villagers; its payment is now almost universally resisted by the Christians, as compliance necessarily entails a refusal of the Sacraments by their Missioners. The same may be said of the poor Catholic cultivators, who are frequently ordered, by their masters, to assemble to drag the large car of the idols, used in the Native processions, all over the country. Much persecution has been suffered on this score, but not entirely in vain, for even the Heathen masters begin to find it to their advantage not to persecute their labourers too severely for following the dictates of their religious duty. Very much suffering has, however, been and still is endured for both of the above causes, and as *custom is law* in India, it is difficult for a man to obtain legal protection for infringing an old established custom on merely conscientious grounds. It will be easily understood by those who have read history, and reflected, that an entire change can never be effected in the way of thinking and feeling of a portion of the inhabitants of a country, without necessarily producing a certain degree of clashing of interests and prejudices. Under the self-interested and careless administration of the Goa Clergy, the Christians had lost every vestige of practical belief, whatever was required of them by the Heathens, amongst whom they lived, was readily assented to; now that they have been awakened to a sense of their duty, their resistance to what was forbidden them by their religion has necessarily produced a certain degree of contention, and hostility, on the part of their neighbours, excited more by the change of social position, than by any dislike for the religion which was the cause of it. Though the confusion of this period of transition is of short duration in most cases, where one party is actuated by charity, and the other unsupported by power, yet the frequent recurrence of such scenes in the various parts of the whole Mission, has produced no small amount of suffering and petty persecution. Yet it is a most convincing and consoling proof that real good has been done, and that religion has made an impression upon the hearts of those who have embraced it.

An admirable plan has been formed by some of our Missioners to procure waste land, which may be had for a very trifling sum, and to establish upon it those who, by their isolated or dependant position, amongst the Heathens, find themselves too much exposed to persecution. An institution of this sort might be set on foot with very small means, and connected with it might be a large establishment for the infirm and aged: devout reader, if you could only know what a number of *immortal souls* would be saved by these means, surely your heart would warm towards the suffering Mission, whose wants are here laid before you; you would cheerfully give of your abundance, or even deprive yourself of some ordinary comfort, to contribute to so holy a work, and thus find in eternity the reward of a temporal sacrifice.

Negapatam is the most commercial town on the whole Coast, south of Madras: it is a part of the kingdom of Tanjore. Close to the town, on a piece of ground obtained from the Government, is situated our Catholic College, which is the future hope of the Mission, as the nursery of good Native Priests and Catechists, and as a resting place for the young Missioners, who come out from Europe, in order to acclimatize them, and give them time to learn the language before penetrating into the interior of the Mission. In another chapter will be found an account of the first establishment, and early trials of this College, which have been so severe as to convince us that a work which has been so signally supported by Providence, under the severest difficulties, must eventually be productive of much solid good.

One of the Fathers, who lives in the College, is in charge of the Native congregation at Negapatam, and another Father takes care of a second congregation about five miles off—the number of Christians is about 6,000. Nearly all the old churches here, as at Tanjore, are in the possession of the Schismatics. The Parish Church is a temporary building, of mud and palm-leaves, all except the chancel and choir, which are solidly built and roofed, and tolerably ornamented.

A few miles to the South, along the coast, is the church of Velangany, one of the oldest and

and finest churches in Southern India. It is dedicated in honour of the B.V. Mary, and has been remarkable as a Catholic pilgrimage ever since its erection; it is still in the hands of the schismatic Priests, though there remains but a very small congregation now frequenting it. There are about 3000 Christians belonging to this Catholic congregation. They have a small and neat church, about half a mile from the old one, but far too small for their numbers.

The Christians of India have been, for some years, in a painfully anomalous position. A small and factious portion of the ancient congregations, still adhering to the Goa priests, who have been deprived of all their functions for canonical reasons, and by lawful authority, remain in possession of the large and handsome churches, which exist here and there throughout the country, many of them well endowed. These churches have always been considered as Catholic: they were raised by Catholic money, chiefly by the ancient Jesuit fathers, and supported by Catholic funds. In what country would a clergyman openly apostatising from the faith of which he had been considered the Pastor, be allowed to retain peaceable possession of his church or chapel, with *a few dozen* of his parishioners, to the exclusion of all those who adhered to the worship for which the church or chapel had been erected a few years previously? Yet such is the actual state of things in India, and were it not for the constant efforts of the Catholic Priests in many places, the irritation occasioned by it would often have resulted in violence and bloodshed.

Several points of the Madura district are remarkable as places of pilgrimage for Catholics; the principal ones are dedicated in honour of the Blessed Virgin Mary, to whom the Indians have a very great devotion, as their principal Patroness and Advocate with her Divine Son. Though the exterior marks of devotion towards the Saints are far greater than Europeans are accustomed to, yet nothing can be more certain than that there is no sort of undue or extravagant worship connected with it, the plainest proof of which is that the same marks of respect and esteem are shewed by the natives to their Catholic Priests and to all superiors whom they very much respect. If time and space allowed of it, many instances might be given of most signal favours received by prayers addressed to heaven through the intercession of the Blessed Virgin; one alone shall be introduced, which may be implicitly relied on, as a positive fact: every one is of course perfectly free to give credit to it, or not, as best suits his own ideas—the circumstance shall be related as it happened. From the village of Manapadon Rev. Father Antony Sales writes to his Superior, on the 20th February, 1841, stating that a short time previously the inhabitants of the village were in great consternation on account of the absence of rain, as the time of the rainy season was far advanced, and the sky still remained pure and blue as at the finest season of the year. The failure of the periodical rains is a dreadful calamity in India, as it occasions the total loss of all crops upon the lands that are not irrigated. Having waited in vain for several days, the people determined to draw lots, in order to find which of their gods was to be propitiated in order to avert the threatened scourge; for the village contained but few Christians. For this purpose they wrote upon pieces of palm leaf the names of the eleven principal Pagodas in the country around, and on the twelfth the name of a small church dedicated in honour of the Blessed Virgin, in the immediate neighbourhood. The people agreed to throw these twelve tickets into the fire, declaring that if any of them remained unburnt they would address themselves to that church, to obtain deliverance from the impending misfortune. This was accordingly done, and, strange to say, the palm leaf ticket on which was inscribed the name of the little church dedicated in honour of the Most Blessed Virgin remained intact, whilst the others were immediately consumed. The assembled people rushed in a body towards the church, exclaiming "Great is the God of the Christians, Holy is his Mother," and before they had reached the church the pure sky began to be overcast, and soon the rain came down in torrents. The billet which had been so wonderfully preserved from the fire was safely deposited in the church. In their gratitude these heathens immediately subscribed a considerable sum for the adornment of the little church, and it is hoped that the recollection of the miracle will dispose their hearts to listen to a Missioner, when one can be sent thither.

The next part of the Mission that merits consideration is Madura Proper and the surrounding country, consisting of the Marava country, to the S. East, and Dindigul at the foot of the hills, to the N. West.

Madura, or as the natives more usually pronounce it Mattura (with a very short penultimate), is situated about eighty miles to the south of Trichinopoly. As early as the year 1842 a handsome church, and a tolerably convenient house, were erected in this city, as the most central point of the Mission, and consequently within reach of several of the Fathers as a place of repose and rendez-vous, to consult about their mutual affairs, and re-establish their health, often much affected by living in the small huts which are their only resting places in the out stations. The garden surrounding the house is one of the most profitable properties of the Mission, at present producing about £7 *sterling per year.* Though Madura is the central point of the Mission, and gives its name to the whole Vicariate, it is probably the portion which has given the least consolation to those who have laboured there. The number of Catholics is very small, and consists chiefly of a colony of weavers, who, as soon as the church was built, came and settled round it. The schismatics count about 2,000 souls, and are nearly all Pariahs. In no part of India converted by the Catholic Missioners has religion suffered more loss than in Madura. It was the theatre of the labours of Father de Nobili, and was the first place where a native of high caste so far humbled his pride as to acknowledge Jesus Christ crucified as his God and Redeemer. The Catholics were numerous, and belonging to the highest castes, but all this has now passed away, and as if in punishment for graces refused, it is now the most sterile and barren part of the whole Mission. In no place did the French Missioners on their return find the morals of the nominal Christians so terribly corrupt, and this is still the great obstacle to their conversion.

The Missioner in charge at Madura has likewise the care of about five thousand other Christians, scattered over an extent of about thirty miles. Within this district is situated Rasakambiram, where is the tomb of Rev. Father Martin, one of the four first fathers who landed in 1838 to recommence the Mission. A short account of his life and death is given in the obituary of the Mission, contained in the third chapter of this work. At some distance is a decent church, in a village which has always been remarkable for its really Christian spirit of piety. In every other part of the district, the chapels and dwellings of the Missioners are mere huts, of the most miserable description, more calculated to excite pity than devotion or respect. The Protestants have a handsome church, with large schools, at Sevagunda, a city which is the residence of a petty Indian Prince. This city contains some handsome Hindoo temples, and large sums are expended on them. The Catholics are in very small numbers there, and their church is of the most miserable description.

Closely adjoining is the district of *Marava,* containing about 25,000 Christians, in a territory of about 70 miles long by 40 in breadth. It is administered by three Fathers. Many of the Christian villages are very close to one another, but most of the churches are but huts of a very poor sort. There are however five small churches tolerably built, either by the Mission or by the Christians themselves, with assistance from the Mission. The congregations are composed of nearly all castes, but the greater part are of the Odean, or Cultivator caste, very remarkable for their religious spirit, their simplicity, and patriarchal manners. The Schismatics in this district are particularly turbulent and active, and have three priests *at their service.* This expression is advisedly used, for the schismatic priests are literally at the service of their congregations, and for money will do *anything* required of them. They possess all the old churches formerly erected by the Jesuit Missioners; the principal of these is the magnificent old church of Sarougani, the largest and best appointed in the whole of S. India.

The litigious spirit and constant aggressions of the schismatics have done more to prevent conversions amongst the heathens in this district than in any other part of the Mission. The Marava caste were formerly masters of all this country, but their influence and numbers are now very much diminished; there are a few Christian families amongst them, and conversions are not unfrequent, which console the Missioners, in some degree, for the numbers of families around them now heathen, though bearing Christian names and descended from Christian parents. They still preserve a great respect for the Catholic Missioner, and many of them bear the name of "*John*" in honour of

Father de Brito, who was martyred in their country and is held in the greatest veneration. The Christians have erected a church and a tomb at the place of his martyrdon, which still exist, though not the slightest trace remains of the palace of the Prince who put him to death,

Ramnad is the next point of the Mission deserving of attention. It is an old Fort on the sea coast; within the ramparts was a Catholic church well built and endowed, which has however fallen to decay. It is in the hands of the schismatics, who a few years ago carried off the church plate and every available thing in it, and then let it fall to ruin. A small hut has been constructed near it by the Catholic Missioner, for the instruction of the native Christians, who are unfortunately very indocile and ignorant. The presence of the Missioner has however produced some good.

Across the narrow strait of Pamben is the Island of the same name, which contains also its portion of Christians, but unfortunately they are so ignorant, and so wanting in intelligence, that it is scarcely possible to make them understand even the essentials of religion. They live almost entirely in the woods, but time and perseverance has produced a good effect even on them. The channel of Pamben, between the island and the main land, is narrow, and has lately been dredged out by the Government, to a sufficient depth to allow ships of 120 or 200 tons, engaged in the country trade, to pass from Negopatam to Colombo.

At one end of the island which forms this channel is the famous Hindoo shrine of Ramasaram, to which annually thousands of pilgrims resort, from the farthest parts of India.

In the centre of the island is the church of St. James, formerly large and rich; it is now little frequented, and consequently poor. It is in the hands of the schismatic clergy, and is visited once a year by the priest of Montonpethy, on the coast, where there is another large and rich schismatic church, with a garden giving an annual revenue of about £100 sterling.

A few miles to the N. West of Madura lies the district of Dindigul, which extends to the foot of the mountains. It contains about 12,000 Christians, of whom about three-fourths are Catholics. The rest still follow the schismatic Priest, who is now in possession of three of the largest and best churches, which were formerly built by the Jesuit Missioners, and which were made over to the present Fathers by the Christians on their return to the country in 1838. They continued in their possession for some years, when, strange though it may appear, they were, by the arbitrary order of an English police magistrate, forcibly expelled from them, and being Frenchmen, their ignorance of the necessary steps prevented their obtaining redress.

Dindigul enjoys a much more temperate climate than any other part of this district, and is within an easy journey of the Siroumaley Hills, on which, during several months in the year, till the rains set in, a delightful European temperature is to be found. The top of the hills is very fertile, and produces excellent coffee. The Protestants made great efforts to establish themselves at Dindigul, and make converts to their theories: for a time—as long as novelty lasted—they succeeded, but now their congregation has dwindled down to almost nothing, their church is nearly empty and their schools are deserted.

The novitiate of the Catholic Mission has

been at this place for the last few years, having been removed from Trichinopoly, where three of the novices had died from cholera produced by the heat of the climate, privation and too sudden change. In 1850 the novitiate consisted of nine young men, English, Goanese, Bengalees, and Natives of the country. One of the English was a convert, a young officer of great talent and promise, who "left all to follow Christ" and embrace the "folly of the cross," through love of Him who first embraced it for love of mankind.

Palamcottah, in the immediate neighbourhood of Tinnevelly is the next station worthy of attention. How many pages have been written, how many reports have been made, to detail and publish to the world the triumphs of Protestant missionaries, at Tinnevelly. It would be difficult and impossible even for themselves correctly to state the numbers of their followers, for very many villages are Protestant only in name; suffice it to say that their numbers are very much overstated, that their progress in the last few years has been very small if they have not even retrograded, for *whole villages have abandoned them*, and we hear of none that have supplied their place. It is even painful to add, though most strictly true, that if the underworking of these missions in many cases were laid bare, and the means used to *force* whole villages to *sign* themselves Protestant were made public, many a zealous and right-minded Protestant subscriber, who has deprived himself of his hard-earned gains to contribute generously to the conversion of the Pagan, would grieve at his money being so misapplied by those whom, in the sincerity of his heart, he respected as the apostles of a holy and self-denying law. As a proof of the want of accuracy in Protestant reports, the following instance may be cited. It was stated in a missionary report that the whole of the Catholic congregation of Moolicherry, in the district of Erichoer, in the Malialam, had become Protestants; the Protestant missionary was complimented by the committee to whom his report was forwarded, a subscription was raised, and money was sent him in abundance to build a church for the new converts. The fact was, that of the whole congregation only thirty-four persons, men, women, and children had abjured the Catholic faith, and for the following reason.

An influential member of the congregation was living in open scandal, and was exhorted to reform and do penance. Highly indignant at the holy zeal of his pastor, he left the church, and immediately repaired to the Protestant missionary, who received him with open arms. Thirty-four (not 346, as stated) individuals, the immediate relatives and dependants of this man, were forced by him to follow him to the Protestant church. The charitable money of the poor and well-intentioned Protestant is often thus applied to welcome and shelter the guilt of those whom the Catholic church forces out as unworthy of her Communion. A close examination of the real results of Protestant efforts would produce a curious disproportion between results and means. As this subject is treated more fully in another chapter, it is not necessary to dwell upon it here.

The Catholic Mission at Palamcottah and its immediate neighbourhood numbers about 12,000 Catholic Christians, all baptised, and most of them well instructed in their religion, The Catholics of this district have rendered themselves remarkable by their steady efforts to procure themselves respectable churches and to contribute in some degree to the comforts of their Missioners, who, on their part, have always been obliged, when any chance placed a little money at their disposal, to assist their congregations to the utmost of their power in enlarging the church sufficiently to hold the encreasing numbers of their flock. The Christians are nearly all very poor, and it is chiefly by contributing their own labour that they are enabled to effect the little good that has been done. Here, as in the other parts of the Mission, there is a great want of schools, for the people are unable to pay schoolmasters, and can with difficulty dispense with the aid of their children in gaining their living. The Christians in the neighbourhood are chiefly *Sanars* or cultivators of the palm tree, from which they extract sugar and spirits.

It may be interesting to the reader to know what is the usual method pursued by the Missioner in administering a Christian Village.

The time of the Father's visit being announced, several of the principal Christians of the village assemble at their little church to welcome him on his arrival, and immediately after all those who wish to approach the Sacraments assemble. After praying for a short time, the Catechist begins the regular instructions on the principal truths of religion; this is followed by an examination of conscience, read aloud by the Catechist, and responded to by each one in his own heart, in the presence of God; then follows another instruction on the truths of Christianity, laying special weight on the goodness and sufferings of Christ, the eternity of a future state of happiness or woe, and all such motives as are most likely to awake contrition in the believing mind; the Priest then addresses a few words of earnest exhortation to the assembled Faithful, and afterwards individually examines each whom he may not remember to have been previously satisfied with, in order to assure himself that they are sufficiently instructed to know how to approach the Sacraments worthily. Enquiry is then made of the catechist and the elders of the village if there are any public scandals, which, if they exist, are immediately enquired into before those whom it may concern; every effort is made to reconcile those at variance, and many lawsuits (a *pastime* to which the natives are particularly partial) are thus prevented. Then follow the confessions and preparation for Holy Communion, which are continued often far into the night. Next morning, Mass is celebrated at a convenient hour for the congregation; all those who may wish to speak to the Father are afterwards admitted, and, thus employed, the day wears on in doing good. One, two, or more days are thus spent, according to the number of the congregation, and when the moment of the Father's departure arrives, the Christians prostrate themselves to receive his blessing, and accompany him to a considerable distance from the village.

The coast of the fishery, so often mentioned in the life of St. F. Xavier, remains now to be described. The line of country so called is the S. E. shore of India, from Cape Comorin for about ninety miles up the coast. It contains a large number of Christians who are descended from the early converts of St. F. Xavier, scattered in about eighteen villages along the coast line. The character given of these people now 300 years ago by the "Apostle of the Indies" is as perfectly applicable to their present character as if it were written to-day. Their turbulent and captious disposition, ever prone to take offence, their fondness for intoxicating drinks, makes them exceedingly hard to govern, and the insults which they heap on their Priests one day, though the very day before they may have been strong in their expressions of regard and esteem, make the Mission amongst them most trying to human nature. Besides this, their churches are of old standing, established formerly by the Portuguese, and they have a sort of traditionary mixture of Indo-Portuguese customs to which they are very much attached, and anxious to require the Missioner to adhere. This sort of susceptibility occasioned a quarrel between the chief of the Caste and the European Priests, which did immense harm to religion in this district. The chief wished to require the same obedience to his will from the European Priests which, by dint of money, he had easily obtained from the Goa clergy. When he found this could not be, he entirely altered his policy, and exerted every means *per fas et nefas*, to dislodge the Catholic Priests from the churches of which they had been for some years in peaceable possession, and re-introduce the Goa Priests. The constant vexations which the great influence of the chief was able to raise, for many years exposed the Fathers to the greatest suffering of body and mind; their patience and forbearance have at length nearly obtained the victory, for five out of six parts of the Christians of this Caste have followed their Pastors, and the chief himself seems inclined to submit at last. If an event so fortunate does take place, it will prove most advantageous to religion, and the erring chief, who by following his ambition has brought sorrow on others and poverty on himself, may feel sure of a kind reception if he returns home to the holy Catholic Church. Triticoven is the principal town along this part of the coast; there is a handsome old church on the sea shore, formerly built by the Portuguese Jesuits, but now in the hands of the revolted chief. To replace it, a large and well-built church has been raised by the Catholic Missioners. It is still unfinished, and will yet need a considerable sum for its completion; but it is much admired by the natives, who have themselves contributed in labour and money to its erection. The entire and uncontrolled possession of this church in so principal a station has produced a most beneficial effect, by bettering very considerably the position of our Fathers in a district where every effort had been made by the schismatic party to throw odium and contempt upon them.

Along the coast to the South, and in the interior down to the Cape, are several other small congregations of Christians which are visited from time to time by the Missioners.

Much more might be told of the present state of the Mission, but it would be impossible to mention all in the limits of this little work. Enough has been said to give a general idea of the Christians, of their present state, and of the way in which is carried on the holy work of leading them to the knowledge of our Divine Redeemer, and labouring for their sanctification by the fulfilment of the law for which Christ died. Much has, thank Heaven, been done, considering the means at the disposal of the Missioners, and the severe poverty to which nearly all of them condemned themselves, has received an abundant recompense in some cases by the devotion and piety of those for whom they were labouring. None but those who have experienced it can imagine what a thrill of consolation, and what a sweet hope for the future, sometimes fills to overflowing the heart of the Missioner as he leans over the dying form of the poor Indian, to whom he feels himself more strongly attached by the tie of eternal love and charity than by any earthly affection to the friends of the distant home of his youth. Experience has shewn that even the most educated and polished European mind can feel a deeper gratification in one look of contrition and hope in the dying eyes of the most illiterate neophyte than ever could be felt in the most brilliant academical success, or the most assiduous court paid to talent in Europe. On the other hand no one who has not himself felt it can imagine the pain of mind which afflicts the Missioner when he sees so much good to be done, and seeming easily within his reach, and which he finds it is impossible to carry out, from want of funds; any one who can appreciate this feeling will not be astonished that it was necessary for superiors to issue positive orders and injunctions to the Missioners rather to spend their little means on their own poor persons, in taking indispensable care to preserve their health, than in futile efforts to do charity beyond their power. In the short concluding chapter a few words will shew how great are the wants of the Mission, and how small are the means of meeting them.

CONCLUSION.

The Mission at present consists of one Bishop, who is a Vicar Apostolic, forty-two Priests, sixteen young Church students, four lay-brothers, and twenty-five catechists. The Vicar-Apostolic is the Right Rev. Dr. Canoz, S.J., bearing the episcopal title of Tamas, in the Isle of Cyprus. His Lordship is a Frenchman by birth, and has spent twelve full years on the Mission, the last four as Bishop, and Superior. For about two years previous to his consecration, Rev. Father Canoz had charge of the whole Mission as Superior, under the Vicar Apostolic of Pondicherry. In 1844 Rev. Father Bertrand, who had been for some time Superior, finding his health completely broken, and being utterly unable to continue his apostolic labours, judged it best to return to Europe, in order to make known the actual state and wants of the Mission. The real necessity of sending some one to Europe made him overcome the scruple he otherwise would have felt in incurring such heavy expense merely for health's sake. On his arrival in Rome, by his able efforts, and the reasons which his personal experience was able to furnish, he established the point that Jesuit Missions could in no way be so successfully governed as by Superiors of the Order, bearing Episcopal rank, and the titles of Vicars Apostolic. Having found means to avoid the heavy charge himself, it fell upon Father Canoz, who was then Superior of the Mission. His Lordship was consecrated at Trichinopoly, in the church of the Blessed Virgin, on the feast of St. Peter and Paul, 1847, by the Archbishop and Vicar Apostolic of Verapoly, an Italian, assisted by several of the other Bishops of India, and a large number of Priests. This was perhaps the largest meeting of Catholic Clergymen which had ever taken place there, and for a few days they forgot, in the pleasure of one another's society, the solitude of their isolated Missions and their long exile from home. During the four years which have elapsed since the consecration of Bishop Canoz, much has been done to organize the Mission and systematize its manner of working. The steady perseverance of the Missioners in striving to maintain peace and order, though under the severest provocation from the schismatics, has earned for them, in many instances, the good will and esteem of the English magistrates. Even those who, by feeling and inclination, were most hostile to the doctrines which they believed to be taught by the Catholic Missioners, were unable to withhold from them that degree of respect which a right minded man must ever feel towards those who are consistent and self-devoted in an undertaking of difficulty and hardship. The mortality amongst the Missioners for the last two or three years has been *comparatively* slight, and as several have arrived from Europe, the number is larger than it had yet been. The greater part are Frenchmen; there are five or six Italians, and but one English Priest. Amongst the ecclesiastical students there are three of English parentage, besides some from Calcutta and some from Goa.* Amongst the lay brothers, one, who is an Irishman, has rendered himself

* One of the English students is the son of a gentleman distinguished for his literary attainments at home, Sir Francis Palgrave. This young man, after a most successful Oxford University course, joined the Indian army, where he distinguished himself for his talents, and after two years became a Catholic, and then left all to follow Christ, abandoning a career of high promise for the apparently humbler lot of a Missioner.

most useful in the College, in teaching English and mathematics, with a degree of system and perseverance which has produced the most happy results. The others are employed in taking care of the temporal concerns of the Mission. The college does not suffice for its own support, and therefore draws upon the very limited funds of the Mission. It has been already mentioned that each Missioner scarcely exceeds one shilling per diem to meet *all* expenses. The following will shew whence these funds arise. The Mission has from money and landed property about £100 a year; add to this about £200 a year for jura stolæ or clerical fees, and the voluntary subscriptions of the native congregations. The Propagation of the Faith gives about 30,000 francs per annum to the Mission, equivalent to £1200, making in all about £1500 for the support of the whole Mission. Sixty-two persons to support and clothe at one shilling per day amounts in the year to £1131 : 10, thus leaving about £370 for buildings, reparations, care of churches, and all the contingent expenses necessary to carry on the Mission in the most economical way. The frequent illnesses of the Missioners would alone have consumed this small sum, were it not for the constant acts of kindness and generosity received universally from the medical officers in India, not one of whom has ever accepted a fee for advice, but on the contrary have many and many a time, from their own houses and funds, furnished the poor Missioner with those comforts necessary for his convalescence, and which his poverty prevented his procuring. The names of many of these gentlemen will ever be remembered with the warmest gratitude. On several occasions the kind-hearted English doctor has taken the almost dying Missioner from his hovel, and carried him to his own house, where, by assiduous care and proper attendance, his valuable life has been preserved, and his health entirely restored. Many of these illnesses, and much of the suffering of the Missioners, proceed from want of proper food, consequent upon their poverty, and also want of proper lodging.

It is not then, Christian reader, for funds to be expended in what may be called the accessories, and much less the luxuries of religion, that the Missioner of Madura appeals to your charity and sympathies. He asks you, in the name of our Lord Jesus Christ, to give him of your affluence, if you possess it, to procure for him the bare necessaries of life which he stands in need of: he has abandoned home, friends and country, at the call of Him who abandoned much more for us; he daily exposes himself to severe privations, rendered doubly trying and fatal to his health and life by real poverty. He begs you to turn your eyes upon the millions of inhabitants in British India still buried in darkness, and waiting for the light of faith to be shewn to them—to turn your eyes upon the thousands of Christians already existing in India, and struggling with the numerous temptations which surround them, of which not the least is to see their Priests in a distress which they cannot relieve, being, with few exceptions, still poorer themselves. In India a man's worth is in general measured by his possessions, and he is respected accordingly; the show of poverty in the Priest is therefore most detrimental to his influence in the eyes of the Heathen, though it is edifying to the Christian, who knows it to be a voluntary undertaking; but even these latter would very much prefer to see their Priests living in a manner more suitable to their position. The Goa Priest, who for some years was the only one known to the native Christian, too often rendered himself notorious for his rapacity and severe exactions. To counteract this it was necessary to act with the greatest liberality towards the Christians, and to require as little help as possible at their hands. This of course has materially diminished even the small sum which might be contributed by them to the wants of their Missioners.

It will be easily understood by a reflecting mind that as a Mission advances, its expenses must necessarily increase, just as the human frame in youth and manhood requires more sustenance and food than in infancy. Twelve years of steady perseverance in an endeavour to sanctify and instruct the native Christian, and to convert his Heathen countrymen, has produced a great change for the better upon the native congregations; a desire of instruction has arisen which must be satisfied by proper schools, which can be set on foot for a very trifling expense. With this a strong desire for *religious instruction* is steadily increasing amongst the adult part of the congregations, a want which can only be met by well instructed Catechists, whose education and training must necessarily be more or less expensive. The Catechist is a most important and necessary part of a Mission, especially in those villages which, being without a resident Clergyman, are only visited from time to time. On his intelligence, probity and trustworthiness depend, in a great measure, the good order of a congregation, and even perhaps the salvation of many of its members. The smallness of the pay which hitherto, in consequence of the poverty of the Mission, he has received, has been a great bar to his usefulness, rendering it necessary for him to spend much of his time in traffic, or some other means for his own support. Often has the Missioner been obliged to deprive himself of even the most necessary things for a European, in order to support his Catechist, whose services were indispensable for the care of his flock. The poor Missioner of Madura, from his cabin in some plain of India, where a mat and a straw pillow are his only bed, whose whole furniture consists of a chair and a table (if he have one), after a long day spent in toil and privation, raises his voice to the Catholic of Europe, and begs him, by the compassion of Christ, to send him the means of supporting his Catechists and servants, whose *self-devotion* is often tasked far beyond the bounds of ordinary virtue. Though the Missioner's own strength of mind is often brought low by the lassitude of his body, produced by too much privation, he feels his own wants less than the wants of those about him; for in India, as in every other country, it is next to impossible to command the zealous co-operation and help of ill-paid attendants. Devout reader, believe that there is no exaggeration when you are told, by the Missioner, that your alms would materially contribute to the prolongation of his life of usefulness There is perhaps no part of the world where the Catholic Church does not more or less stand in need of the charitable alms of her children for her support; but still the startling mortality amongst the Missioners of Madura, which can scarcely be attributed to any other cause than the privations endured, sufficiently proves that, at present, no other foreign Mission is in the same want and need of assistance, for in no other part of the Church has the mortality of the Clergy been so great as one in about two and a half, within ten years. The wants in England are incontestably immense, but at least the personal wants of the Catholic Clergy are in general tolerably supplied: this is not the case in Madura, where there is no sort of fund to fall back upon, and where if by wars in Europe, or other causes, the Association for the Propagation of the Faith should come to fail, both the Bishop and every one of his Missioners would be exposed to literal starvation. It may be said by some that it is a *Jesuit Mission*,—that every one knows that the order is immensely rich, and consequently that the tale here represented is an idle one. The tale must rest on its own foundation, which is *truth;* it would be worse than idle to relate falsehoods which could be so easily contradicted, and the tale being true is itself the strongest possible proof how false is the popular idea of the immense riches of the Jesuit body. It would indeed be extraordinary if a body which, towards the end of last century, was legally annihilated, and remained as it were dead till 1814, could suddenly rise to immense wealth, especially when it is remembered that within the last few years they were, in almost every country in Europe, the first victims of the Red Republican party, and obliged to fly for their lives, and *beg their way*, in many cases, to more hospitable countries. Again, can it be imagined that these very men who have so lately, for a short time, felt *themselves* the greatest need and distress, would now, were they possessed of the necessary means, leave their *confrères* in the van of so holy a cause, daily dropping into premature graves from insufficient support? The Missioner in India has then nothing but the Providence of God to fall back upon, and therefore has a holy right to draw upon the bank of that Providence whose advances ever remain overpaid, yet undischarged in Heaven, for they *eternally* draw down upon the charitable giver the unceasing flow of God's boundless recompense. The charity of the faithful, given for the advance of religion and the support of clergymen, is the best and strongest claim that erring man, in his weakness, can put forth to Heaven; for Charity covereth a multitude of sins, and to none is Heaven more frequently and positively promised than to the givers of alms. In Christ's name, then, a Bishop and forty-two Priests stretch out their hands to those who would regret to see the Missions of Francis Xavier unsustained.

The Sacred Scriptures in the most positive terms assure us of the eternal reward given to those who administer even to the *temporal wants* of the poorest member of Christ's Church, surely a high reward will be given by the Redeemer and Giver of all good, when for His love a charitable hand is held out to support the very life and health of those who desire these blessings only to expend them in dispensing the treasures of eternal bliss to the millions who sit around them buried in darkness.

The Missioner now struggling to live on a few pence a day will, when supplied with more abundant means, be no longer obliged to turn away with an aching heart and a deaf ear from those who beg at his hands, not corporeal food or earthly advantages, but who raise an earnest supplication for the bread of life and the means of salvation.

Many a time the young widow and the tender virgin have sought from the Church the means of retirement and protection, and have, from the very impossibility of extending to them the shelter they demanded, been exposed to the most imminent danger. How earnest will be their prayers for the eternal welfare of those who have assisted them in the path of virtue. Often has the aged Hindoo, long persuaded of the truths of Christianity at heart, offered to leave a home of comparative comfort, provided only that food were assured him,—and still the same painful answer: "It is impossible; we can instruct you, we cannot support you. But cannot you support yourself?" "I want for nothing now," he might answer, "but at the first moment that I declare myself in favour of the Christian law, I shall be turned out houseless and naked on the world."

And the Catholic parent and child have often asked in the sincerest anxiety, "Father, when shall we have a Catholic school, that we may not see our religion exposed to calumny and ourselves to insult," for growing up in ignorance. The same sad answer is given to each, "No one can give that which he does not possess." And yet in this very land, and all around, thousands of English money, subscribed with the most charitable motives, are annually expended on the various Protestant establishments to furnish their missionaries with even the luxuries of life. To whom has the Catholic Missioner in a British territory more right to address his petition for help than to the British Catholics, who, though almost overwhelmed by calls at home, have yet the will and the heart to help the needy? An humble example of generosity is often a striking one: did all classes of the British Catholics come forward with the same self-devoted generosity and systematized charity as the poor Catholic soldier in India does for the support and spread of his faith, much might be done, and abundant means be raised. The hard-earned pay of the poor Catholic soldier has raised many a handsome monument of charity in India, and supported many a priest to whom the Government he served had refused the smallest help. In many places large churches have been built, ground purchased, and a Missioner established by the united efforts of Catholic soldiers. The unseen and all-guiding Providence of God has sent forth the Catholic soldier, apparently on a mission of death, but really on a mission of eternal life to thousands. The grace of God has supported and strengthened faith in his heart, and inspired him to raise the cross in benediction over himself and as a sign of salvation to the Heathen around him. Whilst loyalty has strengthened his arm, and guided his courage in the day of battle to stand by his colours till death, so faith has strengthened his hope and guided his soul in its combat for Heaven, and his death-bed has been blest and hallowed by the numerous charities of his life; he has forefelt the assurance of the value of alms deeds, and how good it is to have laid up "treasures in Heaven where the moth consumeth not, and thieves do not break through and steal."

Could we now behold them in the possession of those crowns which they have gained by their generous self-denial on earth, and their sacrifice of many comforts for the love of God, could we hear their song of triumphant-joy, we should be struck at the greatness of their reward. Could we hear with our corporeal ears the advice their happy souls would give us, how loudly and exultingly would they sing to us, Go thou and do the like.

FINIS.